SCANDAL IN
THE ASSEMBLY

MORRIS L. WEST
ROBERT FRANCIS

SCANDAL IN THE ASSEMBLY

A Bill of Complaints and
a Proposal for Reform
in the Matrimonial Laws
and Tribunals of the
Roman Catholic Church

William Morrow and Company, Inc., New York   1970

DEDICATION

To all those who suffer because a Christian Assembly fails to give them tolerance, charity, or simple justice.

PREFACE

A scandal exists today in the Roman Catholic Church.

It is a scandal of large dimension—a scandal of injustice which affects, in one fashion or another, five hundred million people, the statistical membership of the Catholic Church.

It affects whole nations like Italy and Spain where divorce has been abrogated by Concordat, and even non-Catholics are denied recourse to it.

The scandal touches all those who have contracted or may wish to contract marriage with a Catholic partner. It vitiates the relationship between men and women of good will in all cults and communions.

We have decided to bring the scandal into the public forum, in an effort to rouse the conscience of the Roman Catholic Assembly and its legislators.

In the Roman Catholic Church, as it is constituted today, the communicating member or the non-communicant who falls under its laws has no legal recourse against the law or the lawmaker.

He is subject to statutes that exist, good or bad. No procedure exists by which he can challenge their justice, their validity, or even their doctrinal foundation. He recognizes a principle of authority but he cannot protect himself against its unlawful or injudicious exercise.

Therefore he is forced to resort to public statement and public debate, to rouse the Assembly to assert, conjointly, his complaints and his pleas for reform.

He has both a right and a duty to do this because, as Karl Rahner puts it, "every individual is responsible in his own day and way for the Church and the life of the Church." He has a similar responsibility as a member of the human family at large.

This is why we have written this book. We are very conscious of its defects. It is manifestly impossible in a single volume to advert to all the variations of procedure, practice, attitude and interpretation in an organisation of five hundred million people.

It is impossible—sometimes for diplomatic reasons—to give full credit to those dioceses of the Church where competent and dedicated men are developing an evolved local jurisprudence on matrimonial matters. It is equally difficult, for fear of greater evil, to expose the full injustice which prevails in those places where jurisprudence is still antique.

So we have attempted to walk a middle way. If our complaints are unjust, we stand ready to hear them refuted. If they are just, we feel we have an inalienable right to demand redress and reform.

Morris L. West
Robert Francis

CONTENTS

BOOK 3: THE TOLERANCES OF THE EARLY CHURCH

BOOK 4: THE PEOPLE OF GOD

But there are occasions when it happens that justice
produces mischief.

Sophocles

More light! [*Mehr Licht!*]

Goethe: last words

                    Who said to me,
A foetus in the womb, a puling babe,
"You have your life, but on the condition that
You thus believe?"—No one! Not even God!
So, gentlemen, I say you have no right,
To make terms for my life. . . ."

Morris L. West: The Heretic

BOOK 1

A BILL OF
COMPLAINTS

On
the existing legislation and legal
procedure of the Roman Catholic
Church on Christian marriage and the
injustice arising out of them.

1

THE PARTICULARS
OF THE BILL

We begin this book with three propositions, which we believe to be true:

a. That many of the marriage laws in the Roman Catholic Code of Canon Law are bad laws, derogatory of human dignity and based on un-Christian concepts of the human person.
b. That the administration of these laws through the marriage tribunals of the Roman Catholic Church fails to dispense either natural justice or Christian charity.
c. That reforms can and must be made urgently to remove an open scandal and a continuing injustice in the corporate life of the Roman Catholic Church.

Our purpose in writing this book is to stir the conscience of the Roman Catholic community, so that it may call collectively on its pastors and its legislators for immediate and necessary changes.

We write as believers. One of us is a Roman Catholic, the other an Anglican.

We believe in man made in the image of God. We believe in man and woman, different but equal in dignity, whose companionship in body and spirit makes the primary social unit.

3

We believe in the human community which grows out of the relationship between man and woman.

We believe in the Christian community, the assembly of the faithful, within, but not separated from, the human community.

We believe in the right of any community to regulate its corporate life. We believe in the right of every man to protest corporate regulation which invades his person, his familial relationship, or his dignity as a son of God.

We believe in authority. We believe also in private conscience.

We believe that man is imperfect and that none of his judgments, his laws, or his works is beyond challenge or improvement in the light of new knowledge and increased experience.

"More light!" We all need it. We want the windows open.

2
MARRIAGE—
THE SOCIAL CONTRACT

On the wall of every English register office there hangs a printed proclamation: "Marriage is a union of one man and one woman contracted for life."

The definition is admirable. It says neither too little nor too much. It is simple, broad, yet very precise. It implies more than it states. It attracts meaning, even from the place in which it is displayed.

Marriage customs are territorial and cultural. If you want to have several wives at once—or several husbands!—you have to move to a territory where the practice is legal. In other words, it is the community which makes the marriage laws, though it does not endow the individual with his or her right to marry. This belongs absolutely to the individual.

Examine now what the definition says.

"Marriage is a union of one man and one woman . . ." Man is different from woman. They will remain different. Their identities are not lost. Their rights are not diminished. On the contrary, they are increased by the union, because each endows the other with new rights which neither possessed before. The community recognizes that, together, husband and wife form a new social unit, with added social rights and duties. One plus one makes two. One plus one also makes one.

The union is "contracted." So the normal laws of contract

5

apply. Both parties must be mentally competent. An insane person cannot make a legal contract. Neither can a minor, so legal maturity must be established. Consent must be free on both sides. Coercion nullifies any contract. There must be no legal impediments. You cannot buy a house with stolen money —and you cannot marry if you are legally wedded to someone else—and the contract must be notarized and registered by the community. The community is not a party to the agreement, but is concerned with it, because a new group identity has come into existence within the community framework.

The union is contracted "for life." Whether it will, or can, endure for life is left an open question. Contracts may be broken, annulled, or terminated by mutual consent. Contracts may require arbitration. Still, the intention is clear from the outset . . . a lifetime partnership of a man and a woman.

You will notice at this point that the definition does not state the purpose of the union. People get married for all sorts of reasons—love, money, sex, social advancement, children, loaded shotguns, or simply because they are lonely.

However, in the various formulas of the marriage contract and in their customary interpretations, the purpose of the partnership is clearly expressed: mutual affection, mutual support, fidelity, a sharing of bodies, the begetting of children— all that is hopefully implied by "union," "unity," "joining together."

There is a large element of hope in every contract. You hope that the goods you buy will match the brochure. You hope the gearbox will not fall out of your new car. You hope your life partner—or yourself—will not wear too badly under the strain of cohabitation.

In the administration of contracts, however, hope has no place. There is only legal presumption, which is at least half a fiction—a necessary fiction to lubricate the creaking machinery of community life. When people marry, the law presumes that they know what they are doing. It presumes that they have discussed their differences and resolved them before they come to contract. It presumes that they have the resources to meet the long demands of their agreement.

But when the marriage breaks down, when the burden of the contract proves too great for either party or for both, the presumptions are proved false and the community is called in to arbitrate a termination of the contract, by way of divorce, or separation, and a settlement.

If you accept the arbitration of the community, you accept automatically the terms of its decrees. It is the price you pay for membership and the service of the group. Rough justice? Yes. But then, life is rough, complicated and puzzling, and the community has to protect itself by a pragmatic, and often draconic, logic.

"If you, the married couple, cannot live in peace, we cannot live in peace either. So pay the settlement, break up the unhappy union and begin again—more wisely this time, please!"

Does all this sound too blunt, too simple, too little related to the complexity of human relationships? Does its irony trouble you?

If it does—good! You are face to face with an important fact: what you think about marriage is determined by what you think about man—and woman!

What is man? A thinking animal of unknown origin, with gregarious and reproductive urges, conditioned by a long evolutionary process to the arts of social organization? A tribal creature who exists in various regions in different stages of development, who has devised a variety of answers to the problems of survival and continuity?

If this is what he is, then you must judge his adaptive efforts by their success and not by moral standards imported from other levels of development. And you have no right to destroy his survival mechanism until he has learned to devise or accept a more effective one.

If you impose monogamy on a New Guinea tribesman, you destroy his economy. If you abrogate divorce for a whole country, like Italy, then you are left with a huge number of irregular unions, and a continuing injustice to children who are the fruit of these unions.

Even if you believe differently about man, you are still faced with the problem of social regulation in the plural societies of the twentieth century. What do you do? Homogenize the society with an imposed creed—as the Church tried to do in mediaeval Europe, as the Marxists are trying to do today? Or accept the plurality, accept the Divine dignity of the individual and the right of private conscience, and direct your legislation to a public order based upon the primacy of the person and the subordinate role of the community?

Whichever way you walk, you end in dilemma. The Roman Catholic Church is in dilemma today on the marriage question.

3
CHRISTIAN MARRIAGE—
THE IDEAL

A Christian is a person who professes belief in Jesus Christ as God, Man and the Saviour of the world, and who, after submitting to the rite of purification (baptism), is admitted into the Assembly of Believers, the Church. From the moment of his admission, he is a changed person. He has received a new gift. He is in union with Christ. He has transcended human nature and participates in a supernatural life.

The community to which he belongs is a supernatural community. He and his fellows in the Assembly are united in and with and through Jesus Christ, God-Man. They are the Elect, the Chosen. Their every act has a new and special character.

Their marriage is a perpetual gift of one Special Self to another Special Self. Their marriage is no longer a simple contract. It is a sacrament—which means a mystery. It is an analogue of God's gift of Himself to His creatures. Their mutual life, sexual, emotional, intellectual, is a means by which the Gift of God is perpetuated for themselves, their children and the Assembly of Believers. Therefore their partnership cannot and must not be broken.

All this is a matter of doctrinal definition in the Roman Catholic Church.

As you see, the definition is vastly different from that which hangs in the English register office. The one deals with a

9

natural contract between members of a natural society. The other describes a supernatural union between members of a supernatural society.

And here is where the dilemma begins to show its horns.

The "natural" is what you see, hear, taste, touch—and what you deduce by reason from these experiences. The "supernatural" is beyond physical experience and beyond reason, unless reason is aided by the Gift of God. The "natural" is what we know. The "supernatural" is what we believe, without knowing. In some cases it is what somebody says we ought to believe—without thinking!

Immediately you make this distinction, everyone is in bother. Even St. Paul could not talk his way round or through the practical difficulties of transcendental Christian marriage. He expressed movingly and beautifully the ideal partnership of man and woman in union with Christ, as Christ is in union with His Assembly of Believers. But he could not legislate for it, except in the most peremptory fashion.

The legislators of the Roman Catholic Church have been in bother ever since—and for exactly the same reason. The supernatural union begins as a very, very natural one. The supernatural Assembly of Believers is always embarrassingly natural too. So the legislators have always stood with one foot in heaven and the other firmly planted on our muddy earth.

They have tried to apply the rules of natural contract to what is, at least ideally, a supernatural relationship which is properly not a contract at all but a free gift of man to woman, woman to man, of God to both, of both to God.

The attempt has always failed. Its failure is plain to see in the twentieth century. The scandal of the failure will continue until we come to grips with the fundamental question:

Is a marriage between Christians always and necessarily a Christian marriage in the true sense? If not, what makes it so?

The present answer of the Church is this:

We presume it is a Christian marriage if all the legal requirements—which *we* lay down! -have been fulfilled. If our presumption is false, the burden of proof to the contrary lies squarely on the contracting parties. And the simple failure of the marriage does not constitute contrary proof.

Eminently reasonable, on the face of it. In practice? Let us see how it works.

4
CHRISTIAN MARRIAGE—
THE REALITY

It is a fact of life that marriages between Christians work about as well or as ill as marriages between non-Christians.

There are happy and constructive unions. There are unhappy and destructive ones. There are those which seem to endure in a stasis of indifference.

Assuming that, in all these marriages, the canonical norms have been fulfilled, are they all, in the spiritual and sacramental sense, Christian marriages?

Or, to put the question in the Biblical frame:

Has God joined each couple together in such a fashion that no man may put any of them asunder?

The most conservative theologian will admit that nobody knows with certainty. The country of faith is less well charted than the country of fact. If he is asked to decide a case, he will fall back on the judicial norm laid down by Pope Innocent III (died 1216) that in doubtful cases the marriage bond must be favoured: *favor matrimonii.* This absolves the theologian from further speculation, but it does not solve the human problem of a couple for whom the bond is a destructive torment.

Modern liberal theologians reason quite otherwise. They say:

CHRISTIAN MARRIAGE—THE REALITY 13

We accept the presumption of the law that, once legal requirements are fulfilled, a Christian marriage exists. But we
accept it as a presumption and not as a proven fact. If the
marriage breaks down, there is another presumption, equally
reasonable: that the parties lacked the intention or the capacity to achieve a Christian union. Therefore a reasonable
doubt exists as to the validity of the union.

If a reasonable doubt exists, then the persons must be
favoured and not the institution. There is no theological jus-
tification for the draconic pronouncement of Innocent III.
Like any piece of human legalism, it is open to challenge.
Marriage was made for men and women. We must not chop
and lop them to make them fit it—as if the marital couch
were the bed of Procrustes!

Both conservative and liberal theologians can make strong
cases. They will even agree on the difficulty of legislating for
one of the oldest and most complex human relationships. But
—and here's the rub!—theologians are not legislators. They
can only offer opinions, which may or may not influence later
lawmakers.

Christian men and women who are members of the Roman
Catholic Communion have to live the laws that exist—good
and bad. As things stand now they have no voice either in making the laws or in changing them. They have no recourse
against either a bad law or a bad interpretation. They have
Hobson's choice—like it or lump it! And lumping it, for many,
means leaving the Church, or being expelled from it (excommunication).

So, if one is subject to the Codex Juris Canonici, or if one is
likely to become subject to it by marriage to a Roman Catholic,
it is as well to be informed on its provisions.

For this you need a clear head and a considerable sense of
proportion—and humour!

5
ROMAN CATHOLIC
MARRIAGE—THE LAW

The marriage laws of the Roman Catholic Church fall into two categories: those which are regarded as of Divine origin and those which have been enacted by the Church as a teaching and governing society.

The Divine Law as expressed by the current teaching in the Church is this: Christian marriage is an indissoluble sacramental union contracted and consummated between baptized Christians.

Like all laws, Divine or human, it sounds very simple—until you come to apply it. The Roman Catholic Church applies the Divine Law by means of a codex of definitions, interpretations and regulations administered by courts in each diocese and by a central court in Rome called the Sacred Rota.

It is these Church laws and the Church courts which are the principal subject of this book.

Let us take only three of the Catholic definitions and see where they lead us.

What is a man? Effectively, the canons define a man as a sane and potent male of sixteen years. An insane, person cannot enter into any contract. A male who is permanently unable to erect, penetrate a woman and deposit seed is deemed impotent and cannot contract a valid marriage. Sixteen is an arbitrary age at which physical and mental maturity is presumed.

A woman? She too must be sane, potent and aged fourteen. Potency in a woman is defined as the ability to receive the erect male organ within her body.

You will note that neither definition takes account of the psychic maturity of the person. The Church, which deals with souls, takes small legal account of the psyche. So the definitions are, to say the least, narrow.

If these two narrowly defined persons are baptized into any of the Christian Communions they are legally deemed to be Christians. However, if one of them is a member of the Roman Catholic Communion, the marriage must be regulated by the norms of the Catholic Church. If two non-Christians marry and one converts to Christianity, the marriage is not deemed to be indissoluble. The new Christian may invoke an ancient legalism, called the Pauline Privilege, to dissolve it.

So, having defined man and woman—and excluded a large number of human beings from either category—the law classifies them into three groups, two of which—non-Christians and non-Catholic Christians—are placed at a legal and personal disadvantage in respect of the other. All men are born free and equal as children of God, but under the law some are much more equal than others!

This brings us to legal procedures and their consequences.

You, John, are a sane and potent male of marriageable age, baptized in the Roman Catholic Church. You want to marry Mary, who is a sane and potent female, baptized into the same Communion.

You present yourselves to your parish priest carrying your birth certificates and certificates of baptism. You announce your intention of getting married.

The parish priest is obliged to establish first that there are no *impediments* or legal barriers to the marriage.

You both seem sane; therefore he *presumes* you are.

You look normal physical specimens, therefore he *presumes* you are both potent. He can't really question you about this matter because he must presume in charity that, as good Christians, you have not yet made a test of your capacities!

The birth certificates establish your ages. The baptismal documents prove you are members of the Catholic Church.

Now the pastor should, but often doesn't, work through a checklist of questions, all of them loaded.

Is this a first marriage for both of you?

If the answer is "Yes," then you're in fairly good shape. But watch it! You're beginning to establish a whole series of presumptions you've never dreamed about. You are of age to know; therefore you are presumed to know the nature of Christian marriage and all its obligations. You are of an age to consent; therefore you are presumed to be consenting freely to the contract. The burden of proof to the contrary lies squarely on you from this moment.

If this is not a first marriage, has either of you been widowed?

There's a neat little catch in this question—for the woman! If you're a widow and you claim you're not, your husband can get a decree of nullity later on the grounds that you are "a substantially different person" from the one he married. In canon law a virgin isn't substantially different from a non-virgin, a woman who has had a child is not substantially different from a childless one. But a woman once married is a matron who has passed out of the possession of her father into that of a husband. And the man's right of first legal possession is deemed to be violated if he doesn't know the fact and accept it. This is an ancient Roman concept which has passed unaltered into modern canon law.

Simple loss of virginity is another matter and canon law doesn't take cognizance of it unless the man writes into the marriage contract that he expects a virgin bride and will accept no other. So ladies, tell the truth at least about your previous marriage, because in canon law women are considerably less equal than men!

If this is not a first marriage, did you commit adultery with each other on a promise of later marriage?

If you did, this is called crimen (a crime against public decency), and according to an ancient principle, you're not allowed to profit by it. So you can't get married in the Church. If you committed fornication together, you *can* get married. In fact it's probably better you do! But the question of profit from this delinquency is not raised by the law; the girl who gets pregnant to get her man is fully protected.

Has either of you been divorced?

Answer "Yes" to this question and you're in immediate bother. A Catholic *can* contract a valid marriage with a divorced person. However, the "ifs" and "buts" which govern the situation are so many that they would require a whole chapter to themselves.

Have you both been sufficiently instructed in Catholic doctrine on marriage?

You have? Then you reinforce the first presumption that you are aware of and accept all the terms of the sacramental contract.

Do you intend to have children?

If you say you don't, the Church won't accept the marriage contract as valid. If you say you do, then you automatically close the door to a later plea for nullity—*exclusio boni prolis* —which means that to exclude the intention of children from the contract is to render it null and void. But if you both know you can't have children, or if one party is sterile—not impotent!—and willfully conceals the fact, the contract stands!

And there are lots of grey areas in between which can keep the lawyers busy for years.

Is there any blood relationship between you?
    You can't marry your sister or your brother because that's incest. You can't marry a first cousin, because that's a forbidden degree of consanguinity. You need special permission to marry a second cousin.

Is there any spiritual relationship between you?
    You can't marry your godfather or godmother!

Have you, the male, ever been ordained to Holy Orders?
    If you have, as the law stands now, you can't marry without a Papal dispensation.

Is either of you under Solemn Vows of religion?
    If you are, you can't marry validly without a Papal dispensation. If you're under Simple Vows—a distinction which makes little sense to the layman—you can marry validly but not legally. In other words, you are married but you shouldn't be!

Is either of you under pressure to marry?
    Coercion nullifies a contract. In Italy and other Latin countries many parents thoughtfully provide their children with a forceful letter which can later be produced to ecclesiastical courts as evidence of coercion. It's conspiracy, of course, but in a country where there is no divorce, and in a Church where the canons are loaded against the person, conspiracy is fairly common.

Has either of you made any special conditions about getting married?
    Has the husband insisted on virginity in his wife? Has the wife demanded a marriage settlement? Has either of you speci-

fied an age limit in the other? If you have, you'd better make
the conditions *explicit* now, because you cannot plead them
later, when the bride unscrews her wooden leg or the husband blandly reveals that he is bankrupt. "Let the buyer be-
ware!" is an old and cynical principle of contract, and the
ecclesiastical judges still invoke it!

Even if your pastor has worked you through the checklist
and found your answers satisfactory, he will still publish the
bans, which call upon any member of the community to reveal any impediments to the marriage of which he may have
knowledge.

If the pastor hasn't gone through the checklist—and many
of them don't—it will still be presumed that you could have
answered satisfactorily and you will be regarded as married,
legally and sacramentally, until and unless you can prove the
contrary.

But you're not quite married yet.

Except in extraordinary circumstances, the ceremony of
mutual consent must take place in the presence of a Catholic
priest and two witnesses.

If you get married in a register office, the marriage is invalid
in the eyes of the Church because the form is defective. You
have to validate it in a religious ceremony before you consummate it.

Consummation? That's a neat definition, too, if somewhat
primitive and dubiously Christian in concept. Consummation
means completion. The marriage is deemed to be legally and
spiritually completed when John penetrates Mary in the act
of physical union. Once the act is done—whether rapinously
or lovingly, whether it is done once only and never again—the
marriage is regarded as legally and spiritually complete, and
binding forever before God and man.

A marriage which has not been consummated may be dissolved, but to prove non-consummation to a Church court is a

difficult and highly embarrassing procedure. Of this more later.

It is time now to look at another loving couple.

Charles is a sane and potent male baptized into the Anglican Communion. Jane is a sane and potent female baptized into the Roman Catholic one. They too want to get married.

Charles is an agreeable fellow, who has a set of Christian principles. He believes in marriage for life. He would like to have children. He would like to be married in church—his own for preference; but, being in love, he is prepared to defer to Jane's wishes and be married in her church.

So, one evening, armed with birth and baptismal certificates, he goes with her to see her pastor. He is submitted to the normal, polite quiz. He answers all the questions to his own satisfaction and that of the pastor. Then he is faced with two blunt demands.

First, that he consent to undergo a course of instruction in the fundamentals of the Roman Catholic faith; second, that he will not interfere with the practice of his wife's religion, nor place any obstacle in the way of children being brought up as Roman Catholics.

The first demand he can accept. It's a good idea for married partners to understand each other's background. He wonders perhaps why his wife isn't asked to undertake a course of instruction in Anglican theology. Perhaps he blames the lack on the Archbishop of Canterbury. Perhaps he doesn't care enough to raise the question at all. He agrees with good or ill grace.

The second demand bothers him. The children will be his children too. He doesn't believe in the tenets of the Roman Catholic Church. He doesn't believe that children should be "bred" into any faith. He believes they should adopt it by an act of free choice after the age of reason—whenever that auspicious age arrives. He is in good conscience. He is being asked to do violence to that conscience as the price of marrying the girl he loves. He objects.

The priest is understanding and polite—not all of them are! The priest puts Jane's point of view. Her conscience obliges her to bring up her children as members of the Roman Catholic Communion.

Immediate dilemma. Charles is in good conscience. So is Jane. If Charles bends to Jane, he abrogates a personal principle. If Jane bends to Charles, she marries in defiance of and outside the Roman Catholic Assembly. She too abrogates a personal principle.

The solution of the law? "If you can't agree, you can't get married validly or legally."

Charles's answer? "You're declaring me a second-class Christian and you're infringing my most fundamental human right."

Jane's answer. "I love the man. I want to live with him until I die. And if we love each other, we'll work out a good answer for the children."

Final outcome? Sometimes they compromise. Sometimes they don't. Sometimes they marry in spite of the law. Sometimes they don't marry at all.

Always there is left a whole list of unanswered questions about freedom of conscience and authority and infant baptism and the nature of the marital union and man's private relationship with his Creator, and the concepts upon which marital legislation is based.

Which brings us to George and Emma!

George and Emma are sane, potent and adult. Neither is a Christian. They marry. They live happily for a space and beget children. Then George, like many a good man before him, suffers a crisis of conscience and becomes a convert to the Roman Catholic Church. His wife does not convert. They become unhappy—for religious reasons or secular ones, it makes little matter. George falls in love with a Catholic girl—but of course does not commit adultery!

George now addresses himself to the Church courts for an

application of the Pauline Privilege. He charges that his old wife, a non-Christian, cannot live peaceably with him. He wishes now to found "a Christian household" with a Christian wife.

The court rules as follows: the first marriage contract was a "natural" and not a "sacramental" one. It may therefore be dissolved so that the convert may contract a sacramental union.

So George gets a new wife, while Emma is left lamenting the sudden discovery that she is a third-class citizen in Christian law.

Which leaves a lot more questions unanswered, about natural justice, and divorce in the early Church and the pragmatic accommodations which the Church has made over the centuries to solve marital dilemmas.

6
CHRISTIAN MARRIAGE AND DIVORCE

Divorce means the dissolution of an existing valid marriage with the right to remarry validly.

It is commonly believed and strongly taught in the Roman Catholic Church that a valid marriage consummated between Christians is *absolutely* indissoluble. This teaching, we believe, is open to very serious question.

It is commonly believed and strongly taught that Christ prohibited divorce *absolutely*. This we believe is a dubious proposition.

It is commonly believed and strongly taught that the Church has no power to dissolve a Christian marriage for any reason. This we believe is a dubious proposition.

It is commonly believed and strongly taught that divorce and subsequent remarriage have always been forbidden in the Catholic Church. This is simply not true.

Surprised? So were we when our researches led us to examine the history of Catholic doctrine and practice on marriage and divorce. We would like to lay before you a brief summary of the evidence for the statements we have made above.

PROPOSITION 1. *A valid consummated Christian marriage is absolutely indissoluble.*

The meaning of this proposition is that the band of Christian

23

marriage can never be dissolved, either *intrinsically*—that is, by the action of either or both of the partners—or *extrinsically* —that is, by a party external to the contract, such as God, the Church, the state.

There is no doubt at all that this is the *present official* teaching of the Roman Catholic Church. As such all Catholics are bound to assent to it.

However, this teaching is not *de fide*. That is, it does not preclude the possibility that the teaching can be changed, as was the teaching on usury, for example, in the light of greater experience and knowledge. There is clear historical evidence that the teaching *has been* changed.

PROPOSITION 2. *That Christ prohibited divorce absolutely.*

This proposition has never been universally held to be true in the Church.

On the contrary, divorce for a variety of causes was traditionally permitted by the Church from the earliest times in the East and in the West. It was, and is deemed to be, in conformity with the teaching of Christ.

On this point we quote Archbishop Elias Zoghby, Archbishop of Nubia, Patriarchal Vicar of Egypt and one of the spokesmen at Vatican Council II:

> Whatever might be the interpretation given to the text of St. Matthew (19:9), we must admit that there does exist an ecclesiastical tradition of tolerance, clear and venerable like every other tradition of the Church, which was accepted and practiced by many holy Fathers of the East and of the West.

PROPOSITION 3. *The Church has no power to dissolve a valid Christian marriage for any reason.*

There is a strong and tenable contrary argument in theology which runs as follows: "Christ gave to His Church—the Assembly of those who believe in Him—unlimited power to bind and loose upon earth for the good of men and women who are the objects of His salvific mission. This power, derived from and delegated by the Omnipotent God, extends to all human circumstances including the marriage bond."

There is also clear historical evidence that the Church has claimed this power, has exercised it, and does exercise it by granting dispensatory dissolution in certain cases, even today, by the use of legal fictions like the Privilege of the Faith.

PROPOSITION 4. *That divorce and subsequent remarriage have always been forbidden by the Catholic Church.*

We repeat that this is simply not true.

Later in this book we shall cite the documentary evidence. For the present we shall content ourselves with a concluding statement by Archbishop Zoghby:

> The East has always followed this tradition of tolerance [of divorce] and has remained faithful to it. The West maintained it for many centuries with the *positive approval* of many of its bishops, popes, and councils, and in fact never attempted to condemn it in the East, even after the cessation of its practice in the West.

Having said all this, let us be clear on the present situation in the Roman Catholic Church. Christian marriage is taught to be absolutely indissoluble. Divorce from a Catholic marriage is impossible at this moment.

What recourse is left, under existing laws, for a couple whose marriage has become intolerable?

7
CHRISTIAN MARRIAGE—
WHAT RECOURSE?

Your marriage has become an unendurable mess. What can you do about it and still remain a member of the Church?

First question: was the marriage consummated?

If it wasn't, you can apply for a dissolution from the Pope. Whether you get it will depend on whether you can *prove* non-consummation—and that, dear girl, dear boy, is quite an experience!

The marriage was consummated?

Then you can apply to the Church for a judicial separation. But you can't remarry.

After the judicial separation you may get a civil divorce. The Church will permit you to do this to protect your civil rights in respect of maintenance, property and the custody of children. But you still won't be able to remarry.

Finally, you can apply for a decree of nullity. But before you do, you'd better be clear on what you're asking. A decree of nullity is an official decision of the Church court that the marriage which you contracted was invalid—in other words that it *never existed.*

Of course you have to prove it before you get the decree. And that's a really rough one!

So let's take the three solutions in order and see how you may try to bring them about.

1. Dissolution on the grounds of non-consummation.

John and Mary were legally married in a Church ceremony. For whatever reason they couldn't, wouldn't, but in any case didn't, consummate the marriage. They know they didn't; but to get a dissolution they have to prove it.

Mary is the plaintiff. She generally is. Her complaint is blunt and simple. "I want to be loved, bedded and have children. My husband can't or won't enter me and perform the act."

She takes her complaint to the parish priest. He, poor fellow, can't do anything about it. He refers her to the diocesan court. Here she is asked to make a statement of her plea. She makes it. She may indicate that John is prepared to corroborate it. This is not enough. As the law stands now, the Congregation of the Sacraments may demand the testimony of seven reliable witnesses to the fact of non-consummation and may in fact require *physical* proof.

It may pay to pause here and say that the statutory number of seven is sometimes varied. The physical proof is sometimes impossible—for example, when a non-consummation case is pleaded after the woman has remarried and had several children. Local jurisprudence varies considerably.

But the law can be insisted upon and, on the evidence at our disposal, is often insisted upon. If physical proof is required, the following procedure is laid down in an Instruction from the Congregation of the Sacraments.

Mary is now informed that she will be the first subject and object of physical inquiry. The court must appoint doctors to examine her under a set of rules laid down by Roman clerical legislators. The doctors must report whether or not her husband did enter her at least once after the marriage ceremony had taken place.

Think about the poor girl. At this moment she is one of three things: a virgin with a hymen, a virgin without a hymen, or a non-virgin who has had intercourse with a man other than her present husband.

If she's a virgin with a hymen, she has a good case, obviously.

If she's a virgin without a hymen, how does she explain how she lost it?

If she's a non-virgin, how does she prove she didn't lose here virginity to her husband? And how would a doctor know anyway?

Even if John is a co-operative witness—which he often isn't—there may be the embarrassing and unprovable revelation that he is potent with any other woman except his wife!

Anyway, Mary in desperation decides to play out the drama. She gets another shock. She has to prove first that she's not using a stand-in! Don't laugh! Canon law specifies the proper precautions against fraud.

Mary finally proves she's not a fraud, just a frustrated woman. Now she faces the medical experts and makes a long verbal statement, interrupted by questions, about where, how and how many times she and John tried to make it, and how and why they didn't succeed!

If Mary survives this ordeal, then she is required to submit to a physical examination.

For this a most detailed and rigorous procedure is laid down by the canonists. The decree, published in 1923, runs to fifty pages with a lengthy appendix.

Two male or two female physicians are assigned to make the examination. The females are preferred for the sake of the woman's modesty. If no women doctors are available, the two men will suffice provided they are "reputable, notable for their Catholicity and of eminent probity in their private lives." Non-Catholic doctors may be employed, but Rome often complains about their employment. A doctor who has been excommunicated does not qualify for this delicate case!

The examination room must be well lighted. There must be an examination table with stirrups and equipment "for digital and instrumental inspection."

The woman, the rules still say, must take a warm bath, lasting at least half an hour, before the examination, "which will thereby be facilitated." If doctors feel the bath won't really help, they consult the judge who consults the Defender of the Bond, and if these two gentlemen agree, the lady may be dispensed from the bath! In fairness be it said that this rule is now generally ignored.

The scope of the examination is similarly defined. The doctors must examine all the organs which might indicate that there had been a successful consummation. Particularly they must inspect the hymen, visually, digitally and with instruments. They are to determine to what type it belongs, and the shape, thickness and elasticity of the hymenal orifice. They are to report lacerations, scar tissue, ruptures and notches.

After visual and digital examination, unlubricated Hegar dilators are to be employed, not in fact to dilate the hymenal opening but to measure its exact size. The dilators should be used in series starting with the smallest until, as the instruction says, the hymenal tissue is uniformly distended around the dilators—and so on and so on until it reads like a textbook of gynecology!

Meanwhile, back at the ranch, John is playing out the male version of the comedy. Is he impotent or isn't he? Is the impotence permanent and total? Is it temporary? Is it the result of psychic trauma or physical defect?

If the doctors find him permanently and totally impotent, the diocesan courts will probably recommend a new plea for a decree of nullity on the grounds of impotence. This will save the Sovereign Pontiff the trouble of dissolving a legal but incomplete marriage.

But it will not save the human dignity of Mary and John, who have been submitted to a mediaeval inquisition of their physical persons and a degradation of their spiritual natures.

Some canonists will say that Church law demands in this matter no more than many civil codes. The question raised by these authors is whether a man-made civil code should be normative and obligatory in the transcendental relationship between man and woman and their Maker.

The upshot of it all? If the doctors agree and the judges agree and the Defender of the Bond agrees that John did not have intercourse with Mary, then the marriage will be dissolved.

If they disagree, the ghost of Innocent III will have the final say. He, of course, will favour the bond—and being long dead, can have no further truck with the living who suffer under his ancient decree.

2. *Judicial Separation*

Before you try this solution, you'd better be informed of one fact.

Canon law forbids a married couple to separate without permission of a diocesan court.

On the face of it the law is both bad and silly. It is bad because it deprives married persons of the fundamental right to protect themselves or their children against injustice, cruelty, or infidelity by the partner. And it vests that personal right in a tribunal. It is silly because it is unenforceable and is, in fact, rarely invoked. In England, for example, separation takes place by permission of the bishop or his vicar-general.

However, the law exists and Catholics live under it—non-Catholics, too, if they are married to a Catholic. So let us see how it works.

First a distinction is made between temporary separation and permanent separation.

Temporary separation may be allowed if one partner's criminal or brutal behaviour endangers the family. Canon lawyers say the phrase "brutal behaviour" is intended literally. Slight quarrels, even regular and serious disputes, are not a grave reason. Nor, says one expert wryly, is it reason for separation when a battle develops because one chided the other for some shortcoming. It may also be allowed if he or she joins a non-Catholic Communion. An interesting contradiction here: if a spouse exercises the right of private conscience guaranteed by Vatican Council II, the other partner may invoke the sanction of separation against him. Separation may also be granted if one parent raises the children outside the Catholic faith.

Both partners are bound to resume what the Church hopefully calls "normal life" when the cause of separation ceases, if it ever does.

Permanent separation is allowed for one reason only, adultery. However, even this statement has to be qualified.

You have to prove the adultery before you separate! Or you have to provide evidence for a strong presumption—like love letters to Lindy-Lou, or long absences from the marital apartment, or nocturnal visits to a member of the opposite sex!

More: if you condone the adultery, or diplomatically ignore it, you abrogate your right to judicial separation.

A minor point, unspecified by the canons: what are you supposed to do while the overworked, understaffed and not overly informed diocesan tribunal gets round to dealing with your application?

In the end, whether you separate with or without judicial sanction, you still can't remarry. So, at best, separation is a halfway house, a limbo between the heaven of hopeful lovers and the hell of an unhappy union.

Which brings us at one stride to the hope of the hopeless.

3. A Decree of Nullity

You are in a trap—an unhappy and destructive marriage. The only way you can get out of the trap is to prove that the marriage never came into existence at all.

So here's the problem in a nutshell. When is a contract not a contract?

A contract is not a contract when either of the parties is mentally or legally incompetent to enter into it.

A contract is not a contract when either of the parties enters it under duress or as a result of fraud or error.

A contract is not a contract when either of the parties was demonstrably unable or unwilling to fulfill it from the outset.

On the other hand, a contract remains a contract even if a competent, knowing and fully consenting party breaches it afterwards.

In case you think we're becoming too secular and irreligious at this moment let us remind you that the Church teaches that the spiritual bond of Christian marriage arises out of the marriage contract, and that church courts deal only with the external forum—that is, the facts of the contract! There's a hole in that old bucket too; but you'll discover it for yourself in due course!

Meantime let's start asking you some questions about your competence, consent and intentions in the contract.

Were you both mentally competent when you got married?

There is a madness of lovers; but you can't plead it hopefully in any court. The legal test—admittedly not the most reliable one—is that you were lucid enough to know what you were about at the relevant time.

But George turned up for his bridal night dressed in women's clothes, or he wanted to whip his wife before having sex, or he brought a boyfriend up to witness the consummation, or he informed her blithely that he liked both girls and boys. Was he sane? Is he?

Flora on the other hand preferred girls, but was perfectly willing to accommodate her husband, or she needed to be smacked with a hairbrush to achieve orgasm. Or she was afflicted with nymphomania and was irresistibly driven to copulate with anyone in trousers. Was she sane? Is she?

The probable legal answer would be that both were sane enough to come to contract, though both are afflicted with obsessive abnormalities that might—just might—call their consent or their intentions into question.

Be warned, however, against undue optimism.

Canon law is much less equipped than civil law with provisions and definitions to cope with abnormal behaviour—and short of gross aberration, mental incompetence is hard to prove in any code. For this reason, in recent years, many such cases have been dealt with not on the grounds of insanity, but on the grounds of "lack of due discretion"—the inability to understand and carry out the obligations of matrimony. However, the canons do point out that what happens after the contract is not necessarily connected with conditions which existed before the contract. The burden of proof that such a connection exists still lies on the petitioner.

Legal competence?

Unless you've married your sister—it has happened!—or an ordained priest—that's happening quite frequently now—or your godmother, or a monk under solemn vows, or a person already married, or a baptized divorcee whose husband is still living, or an impotent partner, you can't plead a good case of incompetence.

The area of consent is a much better stamping ground for nullity petitioners.

A marriage is invalid if you were forced or defrauded into it. The canonists put it another way: consent is vitiated by error, ignorance, or moral force.

A shotgun wedding, therefore, is invalid. But hush! Not so fast. You have to produce witnesses who saw the shotgun or heard Daddy threaten to blow your head off! Or you have to produce a coercive letter.

There is another qualifying condition here too. The threat isn't enough. The threat has to produce fear, sufficient to deprive you of your capacity to consent freely. Phoebe was scared of what Mummy might say if she broke off the engagement? Not enough. Daddy, on the other hand, might give Harry the sack and put him on an industry blacklist if he doesn't marry his daughter. Probably enough for a nullity decision. But Harry still has to prove the threat and justify the fear.

Your marriage is invalid if you were induced into it by fraud —depending on the nature of the fraud!

You think you're marrying blond Gretchen; in fact she's run away with a zither player and palmed off on you her identical twin. You'll get a nullity decree in this case. There is an error and a fraud in the person.

You think you're marrying a millionaire. He's told you he's loaded with loot. After the honeymoon he sticks you with the hotel bill and tells you he's bankrupt. You won't get a nullity decree here because you consented to marry the person and not his bank account.

You would get a decree, however, if you had made it an explicit condition—that is, a condition delivered in writing or before witnesses—that you would only marry him *with* the million dollars. By the way, if the witnesses die before they depose or come to court, you've had it.

Your fiancée tells you she's thirty. After the marriage you find out she's forty-five with a face-lift and other plastic improvements. No chance here either. She's the same person you consented to marry—only the quality is different. And a difference in quality does not invalidate the contract. Unless, again, you specified, in writing or before witnesses, that the quality was a condition of marriage.

You marry, in ignorance, a girl who has been a prostitute. You have her, for better or for worse; because the person is the same, though the quality is wildly different from your expectations. Caveat emptor!—watch where you do your shopping!

You marry and consummate with an apparently normal man, who turns out to be a homosexual or a practicing sadist. Here you have a chance for nullity, but not on the grounds of fraud. The person is the same, though the quality is certainly different. You could plead that your husband had no intention of fulfilling the contract, which includes a promise of fidelity. You could plead that his obsessional sex problem rendered him incapable of fulfilling it. He of course can counterplead that you knew his weakness and consented to the marriage in a mutual hope of cure. Or that you encouraged and tempted him to indulge himself. Or, quite simply, that you are lying. If it's your word against his, with no supporting evidence, then, unless the judges will accept your plea that he lacked due discretion, your chances of a nullity decree are very, very slim.

Suppose you marry a girl in the hope of having children by her and find that she deliberately concealed the fact that she had had a hysterectomy. You might charge fraud, but, in default of evidence, the simple affirmation of your wife that she had revealed the facts would destroy your plea. You couldn't charge a difference in the person because a person in law is not just the sum of his parts—unless the parts happen to be the male organs, whose absence makes a man incompetent to marry.

Now, in justice to the common sense which does exist in the Church, let us say that there are many canonists who believe that the distinction between "person" and "quality" is antiquated, unreal and productive of gross injustice. However, their opinions have not yet passed into law—and the injustices continue!

And here are a couple of reminders to paste in your hat:

A widow *is* a different "person" from an unmarried woman. Why? Because an ancient law says she is. So if she doesn't reveal the fact, you're entitled to a decree of nullity. Provided you can prove she didn't tell!

A slave is a different person—still!—from a free man. Why? Because the law still says so. If you marry a pretty girl in Saudi Arabia and then find out she's a slave, you can get a decree of nullity. However, if you know she's a slave but still marry her, the marriage is valid.

Finally, before we begin our long pilgrimage to and through the courts, let's see if we can dig up some other grounds of nullity based this time on the intention to fulfill the contract.

The law governing intentions can be expressed in two sentences. "If you can't do it, you can't contract to do it. If you don't mean to do it, you mustn't contract to do it."

So, if you're impotent, you can't contract to marry. But be warned! There are some dandy legal opinions about who's impotent and who's not. More about this when we come to our case histories.

If you don't mean to have children, if you don't mean to be faithful to your partner, if you don't mean to live with her till death parts you, then the contract of marriage is invalid, meaningless, nonexistent.

But how does your partner prove it? Laws are made to protect the innocent, but all the procedures are loaded against them.

Louis marries an heiress for her money. A week after the wedding night he's off sleeping with a mistress. The common-sense presumption would be that Louis married the girl only for her money. The canonical presumption is that Louis had the best intentions at the time of the marriage but afterwards succumbed to a weakness of the flesh!

Philomena marries the man of her election. She tries sex once and doesn't like it, refuses it thereafter. The canonical presumption is that, though she may be failing in her duties as a wife, she married with the best intentions and must therefore stay married. Common sense and the canons never quite meet.

Ethelbert is a homosexual who marries to have a mask for his preferred activities. Clearly his intentions are defective. But how does his wife prove it, in an ecclesiastical court from which reason and human experience are excluded by statute and procedural rules?

Alfie loves children. Prudence wants them too, she says. But after the wedding she never quite manages to live without the Dutch cap or the IUD or the pill. Alfie swears she never wanted to have kids. Prudence, in tears, swears she was frightened by what happened to her sister after Prudence was married. We wouldn't bet a wooden nickel on Alfie's chances of a nullity decree!

The plain fact of the matter is that Church courts are chary of taking a Christian's word for anything. They argue that all men and women are at least prone to deception when their self-interest is involved. The question which these authors wish to raise is whether it is mandatory or even prudent for an Assembly founded on the charity of Christ to assume the office of policeman in the external forum. The ecclesiastical lawmakers learned their trade from the ancient Romans, who were a thoroughly cynical bunch of practised administrators, concerned much less with justice than with the maintenance of public order.

So here's the logic of your situation, as any Rota judge will confirm to you.

Your circumstances may merit a decree of nullity. You may be telling the truth about them. If you are telling the truth, your marriage is in fact invalid. It never existed. But, without proof, the marriage stands in law!

And that's the hole in the old oaken bucket!

You are married and you're not married. And Mother Church expects you to stay like that because she herself has never been able to solve her own dilemma—the self-created dilemma of an organization which in centuries of matrimonial lawmaking has set the institution above the person, and public order above natural and supernatural justice.

Anyway, there is at least some intention of justice in the courts. So let's pick the plea that seems to fit your case and address ourselves to the legal mechanics of presenting and proving it to the courts.

8
CATHOLIC MARRIAGE— THE DIOCESAN TRIBUNALS

Before we begin this exposition let us concede freely that there are many dioceses where the marriage tribunals are run with extreme efficiency and with the utmost possible regard for justice and charity. Let us state, however, in the next breath that there are others where these conditions do not prevail. So let us begin in a middling bad diocese.

You go first to your parish priest. He's not a lawyer, of course, He's not a judge. He has no legal standing at all. He's just your pastor, the spiritual father of the local Catholic community. He did the standard course of canon law in a standard seminary and he'll probably admit that by now he's forgotten most of what he learned.

He refers you therefore to the chancery of the diocese or to an official of the diocesan marriage tribunal. The chancery is an office of the bishop's headquarters where marriage cases as well as a mass of other administrative affairs are handled. Here you meet Father Tom—a nice old man, or a testy young one or a busy-busy in-between, depending on your luck—and you tell your story.

He tells you there's a legal routine to be followed. You ask what it is. He's not very clear about it, because actually he's been busy with the Cathedral Building Fund and the Knights of Columbus and the Children of Mary and the Provincial Chapter of the Little Sisters of St. James of Compostela who are the bishop's favourite nuns.

You ask for a handbook of procedures. There isn't one. In a really evolved diocese you may get a mimeo sheet of basic instructions. You ask for a legal counsellor. The tribunal of each diocese is supposed to have a list of advocates to assist petitioners. Here there isn't one, because Father O'Hanlon, the canonical expert, is away on retreat or lecturing to the seminarians, who don't need an annulment yet. But Father Tom is sure of one thing—yes, he's quite sure!—you have to put your petition in writing, and then it will be dealt with through the proper channels, whatever those may be.

You ask how you should put it in writing. Father Tom tut-tuts a little. "Just write it down as you told it to me, in your own words. The Church handles thousands of these cases. Our experts will understand what you're trying to say."

The hell they will! You don't know it, but you've just been asked to prepare a legal document—called a *libellus*—upon the form and content of which your whole future life will depend. If you name your plea wrongly, your case may never get to court but may be rejected without a hearing—*ad limina litis,* at the threshold of the law.

Father Tom, to give him his due, probably doesn't know this, because he's been so busy for so many years with the Little Sisters of St. James of Compostela and such, that he's never given a thought to the formidable legal system of Holy Mother Church, devised and revised to deal with emperors, kings, errant princes, aberrant clerics, indiscreet duchesses and political cardinals as well as plain Jimmys like you.

You don't know either—until it hits you like a bellyache in the night—that the Church which demands that you come to her courts does not feel obliged, in justice or charity, to offer you legal counsel, paid or unpaid. You're on your own, Jimmy, unless you find a friendly canonist to help. And where do you find a list of canonists, even if you know the word, which lots of simple folk don't?

So, with or without help, you settle down to draft your *libellus*. You send it to the chancery. It ends, after some customary shuffling, in the hands of a man called the Diocesan Advocate—probably the same Father O'Hanlon who was away lecturing the seminarians. Father O'Hanlon is in no hurry to deal with it. He's one of the old school who believes that a little cooling off never did any case any harm. He's never heard of the ancient maxim that justice must be swift if it is to be justice at all. It's not in canon law, so he may not believe it anyway. Besides, the arbitrary use of authority tends to become habitual in clerics when the layman has no legal recourse against it.

So, some time, often a long time, later, you get a note asking you to supply birth certificates, baptismal certificates and a copy of the marriage lines of yourself and your wife. If you're not living together, you are asked to supply your wife's present address, the name of your parish priest, and the names and written testimony of any witnesses you may wish to cite in support of your plea. By rights all this information should have gone into the *libellus,* but nobody told you what was needed.

Now a silence descends, a long, long silence. Father O'Hanlon is overworked. Maybe the diocese can't afford a secretary for him. Even the judges of the Rota in Rome don't have secretaries. They type their judgments themselves or write them by hand! So this explains part of the silence. Theoretically this is what happens during the rest of it:

Father O'Hanlon has decided, quite rightly, that your case cannot be settled from the documents alone and that it must be heard before a diocesan court consisting of three judges, the Defender of the Bond and a notary.

He has therefore made contact with your wife and informed her of your petition against her and invited her to answer it with supporting testimony. He has, in intervals of his busy life, made contact with your witnesses and hers and prepared a summary. You won't know what your wife or her witnesses have said, because this trial is not like any you have ever known —unless you're a Latin. This is an *inquisition,* properly so called, in which the judges are charged both to seek out the facts and to deliver a decision upon them.

And if the judges decide in your favour, the Defender of the Bond is there to appeal *automatically* against it; but there is no one there to appeal for you against an unfavourable decision. So by law the bond is defended—by law the person is not.

But we're a little ahead of ourselves. The trial hasn't begun yet. And still you may not have been told that you're entitled to an advocate or where to get one. Even if you have one, his use is strictly limited. He cannot be present in court when witnesses are being questioned—*not even when you yourself are being interrogated!* A few local tribunals waive this rule because of its manifest injustice, but the law is clear on the point, and it is usually enforced.

All the proceeding is documentary. There is no verbal argument, no cross-examinations by counsel.

Defenders of the system point out that the procedure has to be documented because canonical courts have no power to subpoena witnesses who may live in foreign jurisdictions and may in fact be unable or unwilling to travel. However, be it said in at least partial rebuttal that the courts specifically exclude the process of cross-examination and verbal pleading. The system is and remains inquisitorial.

Briefly this is the procedure:

The petitioner is called to the court, sworn and asked to give testimony. He is questioned by the chief of the panel of judges, whose questions have been prepared by the Defender of the Bond. His evidence is read back to him and he is asked to swear a second oath, in two parts: that his evidence, as recorded, is true, and that he will not discuss or reveal his testimony until the trial is over!

The same procedure is followed with all other witnesses for and against the petition.

If witnesses cannot come to the court, their testimony will be taken under a similar double oath by an official appointed by the court, even if they live in another country.

When all the evidence is in, it must be printed. Another long delay.

Then—and only then!—can your advocate see the case presented by the opposition. Then and only then can he write his argument for you. But the Defender of the Bond has been there during every interrogation, so when he comes to write the argument against you, he has a big, big advantage. He also has the last word; because after he has seen the printed argument of your advocate he can write a second rebuttal of his own.

To recoin an old phrase, it's magnificent, but is it justice?

He is so obviously a powerful personage, this Defender of the Bond, that a word or two about his office and his powers would not be amiss.

His office was established by Pope Benedict XIV in the eighteenth century "to protect marriage against unlearned, easy-going and malicious judges and collusion by the parties."

His job is still the same, to oppose all claims of nullity.

He is the most privileged person in court. He is present at all interrogations. He gives the judges a list, in a sealed envelope, of the questions he requires to be asked. He can call additional witnesses other than those presented by the petitioner or the defendant. He can demand that further facts be produced which he believes will strengthen the case against nullity. The judges must consult him on every procedural and technical point.

In 1928 a private letter was sent from the Sacred Congregation of the Sacraments to bishops, defenders and other church officials claiming that the defender in non-consummation cases must be exclusively interested in the validity of the bond. This letter said in part:

> . . . Not a few Defenders of the Bond have failed to perform their office properly. For, though they are appointed to protect the bond of marriage, they seem to think that they sometimes have the right to make representations in writing, not in favour of the marriage, but positively in favour of the truth—*an attitude so far removed from the provisions of the law that there is no room for dispute about it.*

Sixteen years later Pius XII felt obliged to contradict this assertion. He wrote:

> The assertion is false that the defender is not as much obliged as anyone to seek the truth. Even today some priests feel that the defenders are, as one priest put it, perhaps unfairly, "too anxious to find for the bond instead of the truth, too anxious to get promoted by winning a case for the Church."

In the last twenty years there have been many similar statements. Pope Paul VI, however, has had something to say on both sides. On the one hand he warned that because the marriage courts work in the name of the Church "they must be above the suspicion of the shadow of any injustice."

On the other hand he warned again that "some unscrupulous professional specialists" may tamper with cases to be presented.

You pays your money and you takes your pick between "suspicion of injustice" and "unscrupulous professionals." The Defender of the Bond is still there performing his original function in Jimmy's case.

Months, perhaps years have now passed. Witnesses were hard to find or perhaps could not be persuaded to testify. The diocesan chancery was engulfed in other work. Documents were missing. The printing took a long time. The diocese was understaffed.

Finally the judges agree that all possible evidence has been unearthed and printed. The Defender of the Bond has written his plea for the bond. Jimmy's advocate has written his plea for the petitioner. The Defender has written his rebuttal. A copy of all the printed documents is circulated to each of the judges. They take time off to study them in between preaching, administering sacraments, acting as convent chaplains and performing all the other priestly functions.

Finally they meet to render their decision by vote. They vote equally and secretly and the majority prevails. One of them writes the majority decision.

You're a lucky man—you think! The decision is in your favour, your marriage never existed! You begin a new life with or without a new partner. Not yet you can't, young Jimmy!

The Defender of the Bond is still there. He must automatically appeal the decision to another court. You didn't know it, Jimmy, but canon law prescribes a double jeopardy for the injured party!

In fact, there's a triple jeopardy, because the Defender has the right to make a third appeal if he wants to. Our information is that he usually doesn't make it. A small mercy in a very rough legal world!

The appeal court is constituted in the same way as the court of first instance, though with different judges. It may decide to deal with the appeal on the basis of the first court's documents alone. It may decide to recall witnesses and call new evidence. If it does, you're booked for another long, long wait. And you're still married until the two courts have decided in favour of nullity.

Suppose your first petition had failed. You would make an appeal of your own. If you succeeded in this appeal, you would still require a confirming verdict from a third appeal court, this time, probably, in Rome.

This would bring you, if you were still alive and not totally disillusioned and despairing, to that court which is called the Sacred Roman Rota.

9
CATHOLIC MARRIAGE— THE SACRED ROTA

The headquarters of the Sacred Rota is in the Piazza della Cancelleria in old Rome. There is an ironic inscription on the portico which dates from the time of Napoleon: "Corte Imperiale"—"Imperial Court."

The word *rota* means a wheel. The origin of the word is doubtful. Some say that in olden times the judges used a round table for their deliberations. Now they use a rectangular one. Some say the word arises out of the revolving roster system by which judges are assigned to cases. The cynics suggest a connection with the mediaeval torture in which the victim was bound spread-eagled on a cartwheel to be flogged or have his limbs broken!

The Rota court is constituted in the same fashion as the diocesan courts: three judges, the Defender of the Bond and the notary. Its procedures are also the same.

If this is your second appeal, the Rota is normally your court of last resort. If it's your first petition, made directly to the Rota, then you have two more appeals, and each time the Rota will set up a new panel of judges.

At present there are nineteen judges to handle cases from all over the world. When we inquired we were told these nineteen judges had a backlog of "about one thousand cases," many of which have been pending for years. Since every case is examined by a panel of three jurists, each of these gentlemen thus has a minimum of about one hundred and fifty cases on his desk. He has no secretary, he cannot even call on a typing pool for secretarial assistance!

One Rota judge made the following statement to the authors:

"I write my decision in longhand because I think best that way. Then I type it. Then I find someone to cut the stencil. Then I have to correct the stencil myself. It all takes a lot of time when I should be thinking. No fourth-rate shop in the piazza would operate this way!"

One case the authors investigated had taken fifteen years to settle! Small wonder!

But a great and ludicrous and tragic wonder that Pope John XXIII could describe the Rota as

. . . having the glory of being the tribunal of the Christian family, great and lowly, rich and poor, into which enters justice to make divine law triumph in conjugal union . . .

If our stricture sounds harsh, let's look at the Rota from the point of view of the petitioner. Your case has been sent, on appeal from your local courts. Or you have decided—if you have the money!—to come to Rome yourself and introduce your case directly to the Rota. To do this you must seek permission from a group of ten cardinals called the Sacred Apostolic Signature.

In either case you need a lawyer. There are presently about eighty lay canon lawyers who are accredited to the Rota and entitled to plead before it.

These lawyers have to be paid. You have to pay. Their fees are regulated by the court. If you can't pay, the court will nominate a lawyer to represent you free of charge or at reduced fees. But *before this happens you must undergo a means test!*

You also have to pay for the translation of all documents into Latin, French and Italian. You have to pay for the printing of all documents and depositions in their various languages. These payments, too, may be waived or reduced after a means test.

However, since lawyers and printers and translators have to eat, there is a reasonable presumption, justified by our investigations, that the paying client will get better and quicker services than the non-paying one!

The judges are not paid by the clients. They receive a modest stipend from the Church. They handle their cases more or less in the order in which they are presented, depending on the readiness of the documentation, which depends in the end on the availability of witnesses and the industry of the lawyers.

On all the evidence at our disposal, the judges are incorruptible. They are not and cannot be bought. They do their best to deliver justice, under the law that exists, the procedures that exist, and the work load on their elderly backs!

The lawyers? Their talent, their zeal, their industry, their regard for money, their care for the welfare of their clients—all are variables. As in every legal system, it is a fact of life that you can get better, quicker and more meticulous legal service if you can pay for it.

It also pays to have influential friends in and around the Vatican. Don't mistake us here. They cannot and do not influence the decision of the judges. But they can and do get files pulled out of the pigeonholes and dusted off and brought opportunely to the attention of the overworked Rota staff—which is already a singular privilege!

How many cases does the Rota conclude in a year? The standard answer is "about two hundred." Which means there is a minimum five-year backlog at the moment of this writing!

One useful footnote. If you're a reigning monarch or a crown prince or a head of state, your case will not be dealt with by the Rota. It will go directly to the Pope, who will appoint a special Commission of Inquiry—of Rota judges—to decide it.

Another little gem: if you're a non-Catholic partner in a mixed marriage, even one contracted under canon law, you can't bring in a nullity petition against the Catholic partner without a special permission from the Church. In effect the Church forces you to become amenable to her laws while reserving the right to grant or refuse legal recourse under the same laws!

So far you will realize we've been dealing only with the procedures of the courts. Now we want to give you some case histories and show you how they were decided, what problems of law and what human dilemmas were involved.

All these case histories are actual ones. Some are taken from official records which are not published until *ten* years after the decisions are handed down. Some were communicated directly to us by the parties concerned.

10
CASE HISTORIES

Molly and Edward, two Anglicans, were married in 1953. The Catholic Church recognizes such a marriage as a sacramental Christian union. Four years later Molly converted to Catholicism. Her husband remained Anglican.

The marriage in all this time was never consummated. Edward was impotent and Molly was obviously a girl who had never been sexually awakened.

Molly described the situation to us in these words:

"My husband was well off. We lived a very comfortable life. He played a lot of golf. I was busy teaching. I suppose I thought that was marriage. I didn't worry about it then."

Later—naturally enough!—she did worry about it. They took medical advice, separately and together. No luck! Edward would never make a normal husband. They agreed, amicably, to divorce in the civil courts *after* Molly had completed her recourse to the Church tribunal.

Molly had a choice of two pleas: the first for dissolution of a valid but incomplete marriage on the grounds of non-consummation; the second for a decree of nullity on the grounds that Edward was permanently impotent and therefore had been incompetent to contract in the first place.

Molly filed on the second plea.

She got her decree in two years from the date of the first petition.

However, from Molly's account of the canonical proceedings, a number of interesting facts emerged.

Molly was rigorously and intimately questioned in the manner we have already described. She was examined by two doctors. The examination proved she was a virgin. However, the testimony of one doctor was rejected because he was not a Catholic. So she had to undergo a third examination by a Catholic doctor.

Edward was never questioned at all. He was not asked to submit to a medical examination. In other words, his impotence was presumed because Molly was an inviolate virgin.

Yet the decree was granted on the grounds of his impotence!

The next case—a very odd one—concerns impotence in the female. This one was started more than five years ago, and to the best of our knowledge it is still going through the courts.

Lucy and Tom, two Catholics, were legally married according to the rites of the Church.

Tom was willing and potent. Lucy, for psychological reasons, was never able to relax enough to permit him to penetrate and consummate with her. It's an oddity, but it happens. The canonists classify this kind of impotence as *relative;* that is, related to a given person or set of circumstances. If relative impotence can be shown also to be permanent, then it provides grounds for a nullity decree.

Lucy, obviously, had some very bad psychic block about Tom and/or his love-making, because, after a year or two, she started a love affair with a neighbour. With him she could and did relax and was very potent.

As a result of this affair, she found she could and did consummate with her husband. However, the marriage was already a failure and it broke up. Lucy decided to apply for a decree of nullity—on the grounds of her own permanent relative impotence.

On the face of it she didn't have a hope. Her counsel—a brilliant canonist obviously!—advised otherwise. His reasoning was as follows: Her impotence was an impediment to marriage. The impediment was removed by an adulterous act. An adulterous act is a sin. A condition cured by a sin is not canonically cured. Therefore the impotence remains permanent.

His reasoning, we are informed, could be acceptable to the courts. The fact that the courts have accepted the plea indicates that they agree there is a case to be argued.

So Lucy could end in the remarkable position of being impotent in law and potent in fact. In which case, having been defined impotent, how would she stand if she wanted to marry again?

The answer is that she was permanently impotent only in relation to her first husband. Therefore she could be permanently potent with her next!

If you think—as we do—that canon law goes a long way round to get some very exotic eggs, try this next case.

Jack and Jill were a pair of married Catholics. Jack was impotent. He could not erect. He could not penetrate. Therefore the marriage was invalid in fact and could be proved so in law.

There was, however, a complication: they did have a child, conceived and born in wedlock. How? Jack could not erect. He could not enter, but he could deposit seed at the entrance to the vagina; and in this circumstance conception is possible, though admittedly rare and difficult!

Could they get a decree of nullity? They could and did under a ruling of Cardinal Gasparri, one of the principal framers of the existing Code of Canon Law.

He ruled as follows: a child conceived thus is born as if from non-matrimonial intercourse and from impotent parents.

So a man can be a father in fact and impotent both in fact and law!

It is time here to point to a paradox. There is no firm definition of potency in canon law. The generally accepted test of potency in the male is that he must be able to erect, penetrate and deposit seminal fluid in a woman.

Pope Sixtus V ruled that a castrated man—that is one whose testicles had been removed—could not marry, even if he could still erect and penetrate his wife.

The fact that he could not produce seminal fluid debarred him absolutely.

On the other hand, a woman who can receive a man is deemed potent even if she has had a full hysterectomy and therefore cannot ovulate or conceive.

To quote a line from a Broadway show, "Women, you see, are different from men!"

The most conservative canonist in the world will admit the contradiction in the law. So far no church legislator has felt obliged to remove it!

The next case is a matter of public record. It has still not been settled. It does, however, illustrate how badly procedures can be bungled by ignorance, indifference, or lack of pastoral concern and how much injustice can be inflicted on an honest petitioner.

Carol had been married only a few days to Patrick when she knew something was very wrong.

It was weeks before she could bring herself to go to her family to discuss it, months before she summoned courage to visit a psychiatrist and tell him the facts.

Patrick was a sexual psychopath.

After her own consultation, Carol managed to persuade him to visit a psychiatrist. This expert called in other consultants. They confirmed that Patrick was mentally unbalanced, sexually perverted, sadistic, masochistic.

It was remotely possible, though unlikely, they said, that he might be brought back to something like a normal condition if he would take a long course of treatment. Patrick refused to consent to treatment. Carol decided to separate from him and to petition the Church for an annulment.

At the diocesan chancery she told her story to a clerical official. She sat there while the priest, lacking any office help, typed out her statement himself. She signed the last page. He wouldn't give her a carbon copy.

Carol went home and waited. The months passed. Now and then she telephoned: was anything happening? Inquiries were being made. Was there a case for nullity which the Church might pursue? The priest wouldn't give an opinion. Could she help with any further information? We'll call you if you're needed.

Always the tone was noncommittal, indifferent.

To Carol one thing seemed strange: she had filed a petition hinging on her husband's psychiatric condition, a highly technical series of medical phenomena, yet officials at the diocese had not asked to see any medical reports or to talk to the doctors themselves.

By now Carol had become wary of asking questions or making suggestions. She kept silent.

Almost a year after her original approach to the diocese she received a call about the medical evidence. The diocesan advocate asked her to have the doctors turn over their psychiatric reports to them.

Several more months passed. Then a letter reached Carol to say that her story, the medical evidence and the results of the diocesan inquiry all had been reviewed in the chancery and that her petition had been rejected. The letter ended: "After much deliberation I can only ask you to abide by the will of Almighty God in this matter." The chancery neglected to mention how they had determined what the will of Almighty God was!

They also didn't tell her what had really happened. The chancery had decided that they could not or would not try the case, which, therefore, had been rejected *ad limina litis.*

This can and does happen when people have no legal counsel. They may have good grounds for a plea, but the grounds are not contained or are not properly expressed in their first agonized document.

In canon law—as in all Latin laws—form sometimes carries more weight than content or intent. But how would Carol —a non-legal Anglo-Saxon—even begin to guess at this fact? And with an indifferent or hostile chancery, who would feel bound to inform her?

Carol, however, was still wondering how she was meant to "abide by the will of Almighty God."

Finally she sat down and composed a long letter to the Archbishop. No answer from His Grace. Two months later came a note from the chancery, asking her to call. She called. She made some tart remarks about her right to be heard in court. She indicated that if the Church refused to hear her case, she would present it to a civil tribunal—and leave the Church.

Action at last! The tribunal would hear her case. But she must make a formal petition. She'd already done that! No, not in proper form. What should the form be? Get a canon lawyer. Who are the available lawyers in this diocese? We have a list somewhere; we'll try to find it. Why wasn't she told months and months ago that she could use a lawyer? The answer was that she hadn't asked!

Finally she prised out of the chancery all the procedural information—and a warning that her case was a poor one anyway and that she'd probably lose it!

In this, at least, the chancery was wholly and rightly frank. Petitions based on mental and sexual abnormalities are notoriously hard to win under canon law. Here are some of the reasons why:

There is no canonical definition of insanity. It's hard in any jurisdiction to equate abnormality with insanity. Therefore Carol could not prove mental incompetence in the contract.

She could not prove non-consummation—even though Patrick had had only one normal act with her and thereafter demanded anal, oral, or sadistic satisfactions.

She obviously couldn't prove impotence. She couldn't prove error in the person. She couldn't prove fraud, because Patrick could countercharge that Carol knew his vices and consented to marry him in spite of them.

The plea she finally made was that the marriage was invalid because of a defect of consent on Patrick's part. In other words, because of Patrick's obsessional sex drives, he could not promise what he could not in effect perform.

Our last information was that Carol's case is still in the first hearing and that her hopes of a favourable verdict are, at best, distant.

Our comment. More and more is becoming known about psychosexual aberrations, but nothing is being done to reform the canons in the light of this new knowledge. Justice? Surely not. Christian morality? Protection of the bond? There are moments when the legal hairsplitting sounds like a blasphemy!

Another case from our files:

Donald and Moira, two Anglicans, were married in a Church ceremony in London in 1950. They had mutually agreed not to have children.

After a few years Moira deserted Donald, who then divorced her on the grounds of adultery. Moira went to Portugal and remarried. Eventually Donald fell in love with a Catholic girl, Ruth. Together they went to consult a Catholic priest about their situation.

The priest was firm on two points. The Anglican marriage was a valid, sacramental marriage. It was not dissolved by desertion, adultery, divorce, or the remarriage of one of the partners. If, however, there was an invalidating defect to the marriage, then Donald could apply for a decree of nullity and, if he got it, marry Ruth.

The exclusion of children did, on the face of it, constitute such an invalidating defect. However, Donald would have to prove it. Before he could prove it, he would have to have permission from Rome to open the case. As an Anglican Christian he was still a second-class citizen.

The priest offered to open the matter with the diocesan

chancery and with the Roman authorities. Meantime Donald wrote to his former wife and asked her to affirm in writing the fact of the exclusion of children from their contract. She agreed to do it.

Plain sailing from here on? Not at all.

In February 1964, working with his priest friend, Donald prepared his petition and delivered it to the local chancery. A month later it was sent back for changes in form. The changes were made. The petition went to Rome. Four months later Rome granted permission for the case to be heard.

Here is Donald's account of what happened afterwards:

. . . Then it began to get complicated. The chancery wrote to Portugal, where a local priest interrogated my ex-wife. There was endless correspondence about the difficulty of getting a competent interpreter in her village. Our priest friend offered to go to Portugal to interrogate her in English. His offer was not accepted. For nine months after that nothing happened. I wrote personally to the Apostolic Delegate in England asking him to intervene. I got a charming letter saying it was a domestic matter and had nothing to do with him.

I went directly to see the bishop. The bishop told me the reason for the delay: his office was hopelessly overworked and understaffed. This was in April. Finally the diocese agreed to begin court proceedings on September 30. I gave my evidence and was questioned. Then they told me that they wanted my wife's evidence retaken in England. They were worried about "the perils of translation." My wife said she couldn't come from Portugal. We were stalled again. When we complained, we were told bluntly that the chancery only had a certain amount of time to devote to marriage cases.

Our priest friend kept pressing the bishop for action. Finally he delivered to us an incredible report: "The bishop says all marriage court business is at a standstill. He suggests we reopen the case with another diocese!"

The end of the story? Donald and Ruth despaired of justice and got married in a registry office. The priest admitted Ruth to communion because as he put it: "It's not her fault if the Church can't make up its mind or cannot dispense justice for lack of manpower!"

Another one? This, too, is from our records.

John and Emily, both Catholics, married according to the rules of Mother Church. John had had a very rigid Catholic upbringing and a remarkably good education—his testimony is precise and reveals a close acquaintance with civil and canon law.

The marriage was not a notable success. Emily had little interest in sex. At one time she refused intercourse for two years. She had two children by John and then declined to have any more. John remained faithful to her throughout, but his tolerance wore very thin.

Finally he decided to take her abroad in an effort to revive their relationship. He applied for passports—and, for the first time, held his wife's birth certificate in his hands. She was ten years older than the age she had inscribed on the marriage register! John understood that the union was a hopeless failure and that his years of tolerance had been to no purpose. The marriage deteriorated quickly after that.

John went to his confessor for advice. He produced the documentary evidence of his wife's deception. He revealed the reason for it: during the engagement he and his fiancée had discussed the question of the disparity of age between husband and wife, and he had made it clear that he didn't want to marry a woman older than himself. Obvious question: Couldn't he see how old she was? His answer: No, I couldn't. I didn't. And love is blind anyway!

The confessor's answer: "If you did make her age an explicit condition of marriage and she concealed her true age, then you are not in fact married. You have two choices: validate the marriage by an act of consent now, or end it now by separation because you must not cohabit with a woman to whom you are not married. Then you must apply, in the external forum of the courts, for a nullity decree, to ratify legally the nullity which exists in fact."

So John, secure in conscience that he was not married, separated from his wife and set about getting a nullity decree.

At the chancery the following dialogue took place. John, a meticulous fellow, recorded this too.

"My confessor tells me I have a right to petition for nullity. How do I go about it?"

"You file a petition."

"Where?"

"Here at the chancery."

"In what form?"

"Any form you like."

"What are my rights in front of the court?"

"You'll be informed in due course."

"Who will advise me?"

"Anyone you choose."

"How do I specify the grounds of the petition?"

"You specify the grounds you think you have."

This took John back to square one: his confessor. The confessor, strong on moral theology but weak on canon law, gave John his opinion: "Your wife is a substantially different person in law from the person she claimed to be. That's the core of your plea."

In fact the confessor was wrong. Under the law the "quality" was different, but not the "person." But John filed the petition in good faith.

He got his answer in three months. Very quickly indeed! His petition had been denied but he did have the right of appeal. We have seen this letter. It omits a very important piece of information: that the case had never been brought to trial but had been rejected out of hand—*ad limina litis*. It failed also to inform John of the reasons for rejection.

So John, ill advised by his confessor, not informed by the court of the true situation of his case, filed his appeal on the same grounds.

After another three months he received a letter—briefer than the first—saying that his appeal had been denied. No reasons were given for the denial. No mention that a trial had not been ordered. No mention either of his right to a final appeal to the Rota.

Was the information deliberately withheld? John, still a tolerant fellow, doesn't claim this. But—a well-trained moralist and not a bad legalist by now—he does claim that the neglect to deliver the information constituted a grave negligence, a breach of justice and charity.

At all events, without knowing how or why, John was beaten before he began. So he began a course of private study on canon law, and when he understood how badly he had been misdirected, he decided to go to Rome to invoke the Right of the Pilgrim, a procedure now abolished, and be tried before the Rota.

It took him five years to scrape up the money. In Rome he consulted a distinguished Rota lawyer, a layman. The lawyer laid down the grounds of a new plea, based this time on defect of consent. The core of the plea was as follows:

"I consented to marry this woman believing her to be of the age she told me. I would not have married her, and she knew I would not have married her, had I known her true age. In other words, I made her age an explicit condition of contract."

John then asked about his chances. The lawyer's reply was clear: "If you can prove the plea, you will get a decree of nullity."

Then they settled down to weigh the evidence. The deception was clear. The marriage register, signed by the wife, carried a false age. But the reason why she had falsified it was the nub of the case.

John had neither documents or witnesses to prove his claim.

Would his wife corroborate his story? No, she had made it clear she would be a hostile witness and would produce other hostile witnesses. So the court would weigh the false document against the wife and her witnesses. If the judges remained in doubt, the bond would be favoured.

How long would the case take? The lawyer was honest. A doubtful one like this, with witnesses in another country—five, six, seven years, perhaps more. How much would it cost? It would be expensive, unless John wanted to apply for a means test. And that, too, would take time. The lawyer advised John to think it over before committing himself to a long, costly and doubtful journey.

He thought it over very carefully. He concluded as follows: In conscience—that is, in fact—he was not married. He might or might not be able to prove it under a law whose norms and presumptions and procedures were all loaded against him. He would go no further.

He is now divorced from his first wife, married to another Catholic—in a civil ceremony. He remains a Catholic. He has no doubt in conscience about his present marriage. He communicates privately because he believes he has a right to do so and his confessor concurs—on the grounds that the Church has no right to compound the injustice already inflicted by its own defective laws.

The next case is an odd one on a number of counts.

In 1940, Sophie, an American Catholic, married Stephen, a non-baptized Englishman, in a Catholic ceremony. To marry him validly she needed a dispensation from the Church. There is no record of the dispensation having been granted. However, there is a record that Stephen was baptized a week later, in the same Church, by the priest who performed the marriage. So in the priest's view at least the marriage must have been legally performed.

The marriage didn't last. Sophie went back to America and divorced Stephen. Some years later, without revealing her first marriage, she married a Catholic in a Catholic ceremony.

None of this makes Sophie a particularly appealing character. However, her second marriage turned out happily and several children arrived. Sophie apparently mellowed and matured and began to take stock of her conscience. In the eyes of the Church her second marriage wasn't a marriage at all. There was an impediment—her first marriage to Stephen. To regularize her position, she had to prove that this marriage never existed!

So, nineteen years after the first marriage, eighteen years after the divorce, fifteen years after the second marriage, Sophie set about tidying her conscience and her legal position in the Church.

One of the impediments to Catholic marriage is called disparity of cult. It means that a Christian cannot marry a non-Christian without special permission. A non-Christian, for the purpose of the law, means any non-baptized person. In Sophie's case there were *no records* to show that permission had been given. There was, however, a strong presumption that there must have been a permission because the priest did marry them and baptize Stephen later. Remember, however, what we told you before. In Latin law the form is often stronger than the content or intent. And in this case the form outweighed the presumption. There was no document of dispensation—therefore there was no dispensation.

By the way, Stephen didn't figure in all this at all. He had disappeared. No one knew where he was. But from out of left field there suddenly appeared—Stephen's stepmother. The chancery court had dug her out of the archives. She claimed that she knew Stephen had been baptized. But she didn't know where or when. No one could trace any documentation on this either.

So the judges were faced with insoluble doubt. They invoked the norm of Innocent III and declared that Sophie's first marriage was valid and the second one invalid.

The case went on appeal to a second court and to a third. The second and third courts found in favour of Sophie—on the grounds that though doubt existed, the doubt was in Sophie's favour and the benefit of the doubt should be given in favour of the welfare of a thriving Christian family.

The decision was humane and pragmatic. Some legalists are inclined to regard it as dubiously canonical. It is the belief of these writers that *all* reasonable doubt should be resolved in favour of the person whether or no a "thriving Christian family" is involved!

Finally, a love affair with a curious end:

Ernest, a non-Catholic, married Hermione, a Catholic, in a registry office. The marriage was invalid because of defect of form. However, they lived together happily and had several children.

Then Hermione had a serious accident and was taken to a hospital. Afraid of dying in bad conscience, she called a priest and her husband. A marriage ceremony was performed according to all the rites and requirements of Mother Church. They were now validly married.

Hermione stayed in the hospital for several months and by the end of her stay had fallen hopelessly in love with a Catholic doctor. She filed a petition for annulment on the grounds that her marriage to Ernest had never been consummated!

The petition was granted. Why? Only the second marriage was the valid one. And Hermione proved that she had been incapacitated by illness, had spent all her time in a hospital bed in a public ward and couldn't possibly have had intercourse with Ernest during that time!

The morality of her action did not come into question, only the physical facts. Hermione married her new man in a legal, valid, sacramental union!

We could multiply such case histories to boredom—and sometimes to nausea. Any canonist could present you with hundreds more complicated and more meticulously reasoned than those we have set down. Our purpose has been served if we have given you some clear idea of the legal concepts on which canon law is based, the dilemmas and contradictions which arise out of these concepts—and what may happen to you if you ever get involved in the legal system of the Church.

In the next chapter we'd like to enlighten you on some legal and theological oddities called privileges.

11
PRIVILEGED PEOPLE

Under the marriage laws of the Catholic Church, every baptized person is a Christian; every unbaptized person is a non-Christian.

The baptized person is entitled to a privilege under the law. A non-baptized person does not enjoy this privilege and has no recourse against its invocation.

The privilege in this case is divorce—a real divorce with right to remarry! The name of the privilege is the Privilege of the Faith. The Privilege of the Faith is subdivided into two parts: the Pauline Privilege and the Petrine Privilege.

Here is how they are applied:

1. *The Pauline Privilege*

Two non-Christians marry according to the usages of their own society. One becomes a Christian. If he can prove that his partner is an obstacle to the practice of his new faith, he can petition for a dissolution, which, if granted, permits him to remarry.

Since the non-Christian has no recourse by way of defense or counter-petition, the word "privilege" is well used. It is somewhat harder to claim that justice is well served!

2. *The Petrine Privilege*

A chieftain in a polygamous society in New Guinea has six wives. He converts to Christianity. Polygamy is not permitted under the Christian dispensation. What does he do?

He may choose any one of his existing wives, or another woman, and marry her under the Christian law. He is obliged in justice to make economic provision for the rejected wives, but the privilege of choice is his, by virtue of his new faith, and the rejected wives have no appeal from his choice.

However, the Petrine Privilege goes much further than this. Its operation is best illustrated by the famous Helena case.

The Helena in question is the capital of Montana, U.S.A. Here in 1919 an unbaptized man married an Anglican woman. The marriage was consummated. A year later he divorced her in a civil court action.

Then he informed the parish priest that he wanted to join the Catholic Church and marry a Catholic girl. His first marriage was legitimate in the eyes of the Church; therefore it was not regarded as dissolved by the civil divorce action.

The bishop of Helena took up the case and presented it to Rome. After four years of inquiry and correspondence, the reigning Pope issued a decree *dissolving* the first marriage "in favour of the Faith."

The legitimacy of the first marriage was clear.

The dissolution was in fact a divorce, granted to a newly baptized Catholic.

So the Church does claim and does exercise the power to grant a divorce and permit remarriage.

To do so—and still preserve the questionable proposition of the absolute indissolubility of Christian marriage—the Church has created a curious theological and legal fiction: "natural marriage" as opposed to "sacramental marriage."

"Natural marriage" is defined as a legitimate union between non-Christians—still called "infidels" in the Code—or as a legitimate union between a Christian and a non-Christian.

Now let us be very fair. Every code of human laws contains "fictions" of one kind or another. These fictions are in fact a pragmatic accommodation to existential human conditions. A joint stock company is such a fiction. A corporate entity is created which then enjoys existence as a legal person, which can enter into contracts and be sued. Presumption of death creates another such fiction. A man who is happily lusting in Acapulco is legally dead in New Orleans. We have already seen how a man or a woman can be legally impotent and yet powerfully potent at the same time.

One problem with such legal fictions in the Church is that once they are promulgated under the magisterium of the Assembly, the theologians and—let's say it bluntly—the pastoral propagandists set about justifying them with an intricate and highly acrobatic logic so that in time they assume a pseudo-sacral character and become so inextricably interwoven with the fabric of tradition that they are deemed beyond challenge.

An even greater problem is that such fictions—being often mutually contradictory—expose the Christian lawmaker to the justifiable suspicion of verbal and legal dissimulation.

Thus the "natural law"—another old and not unuseful fiction—obliges all men and women to render justice to each other in equal measure. To contradict and override "natural law" with a fiction of "privilege" is, to say the least, a questionable procedure.

Another question, much more fundamental, seems to need a very open discussion:

"How can a man be a Christian and a non-Christian at the same time?"

Ridiculous? Not at all. It arises every day out of the practice of infant baptism.

It is the present official teaching of the Church that the sacramental (= mysterious) rite of baptism confers upon the infant the Gift of Faith and lifelong membership of the Assembly of Believers. The Gift and the membership are conferred by the rite itself and not by the infant's own consent—because he is incapable of consenting to anything at that moment.

However, the child may grow up, through a variety of circumstances, ignorant of his incorporation into the Church, deprived of any Christian education and possibly as a member of a non-Christian community. He may reject the Faith consciously and of set purpose. Is he, in either case, a Christian? He says he is not. Common sense says he is not. The law says he is. And the marriage law will treat him as a Christian without requiring him to make an act of conversion or recantation of his non-Christian belief. It will treat his marriage to a Christian as a Christian marriage.

It's another interesting dilemma created by the attempt to legislate for two different worlds in a single codex!

And that brings us to a final curiosity of Catholic pastoral practice in which dissimulation and absurdity are about equally mixed.

12
THE BROTHER AND SISTER ACT

If a man and woman have contracted a marriage which is invalid in the eyes of the Church and which cannot be regularized by canonical recourse, they are obliged to separate.

If, however, such a separation would be cruel or impractical because of age, health, children, or poverty, the Church will permit them to stay together, continue to represent themselves as married, and receive the sacraments—on one major condition: they must not have sexual intercourse!

Most moralists with a sense of humour will agree that the arrangement is a very backhanded way of offering salvation— or of pacifying a couple who have been unable to get justice in the canonical courts.

Moralists with a knowledge of history will quote legislation in the early Church which was much more humane in that it tolerated full cohabitation and readmitted the couple as communicants after a period of penance. We shall cite some of this evidence in the second part of this book.

All moralists will agree that dissimulation is involved. Some justify it as a legitimate device to avoid scandal. Others reject the idea of scandal in today's permissive society. However, the Church certainly compounds the dissimulation by the rules she attaches to this dubious privilege.

If you wish to avail yourself of it, here are the requirements.

You present yourself to your parish priest. You engage, under oath, that you will remain celibate, making no gesture towards conjugal life; that you will so arrange your domestic life that you will avoid the grave peril of falling into bed with each other; that you will cause no community scandal; that you will assure your confessor four times a year that you have kept your oath; that you will take communion in a parish where you are not known.

In our researches for this book we came across only two couples who had tried this arrangement. One couple assured us that they had accommodated satisfactorily. They were, however, noticeably addicted to alcohol. The other couple confessed they had lived it for a while and had finally given it up as a moral impossibility. This couple now receives the sacraments at the hands of a tolerant priest who invokes a much older practice and tradition in the Church to justify his actions.

We have one comment to make. We believe that by abolishing older, more tolerant but still legitimate practices, by adopting certain rigorist interpretations of theology into her present official teaching, by lending or appearing to lend to certain pastoral pronouncements an authority which they do not have in fact, the Church has finally backed itself into a corner from which she can only get out by the kind of lunatic logic which we have discussed in some of these pages.

"If this is religion," said one exasperated pastor, "then I'm all for joining the infidel, who at least have common sense and compassion."

13
THE CASE FOR
THE COMPLAINANTS

We have stated the grounds of complaint. We have adduced, we think, sufficient evidence to entitle us to a hearing by the Assembly. Now we depose as follows:

1. *The concepts of the human person, upon which canon law is based, are incomplete, outmoded, sometimes contradictory and in certain particulars un-Christian.*
    Man is what he is. He is not what a law says he is.
    Man is not an assemblage of physical parts. Neither is he an accretion of psychic qualities.
    Man is an animal, existing in a physical dimension of time and space. He is an animal who knows, who knows that he knows, who is capable in varying degrees of ordering himself in relation to his ambience, to other beings and to the Source of Being.
    Man is a unique being. He recognizes a unity—a oneness—in himself. He recognizes a oneness in the other selves with whom he lives. He recognizes diversity too—diversity in his own self, diversity in the other selves. Not all his faculties are equally developed. Not all the other selves have developed as he has.
    Many men make an assembly, but the assembly never makes a man. Neither can the assembly abstract the qualities of many

men and create from them a new man—a legal man, a corporate man, a Christian man, a non-Christian man.

Many sciences can make valid statements about man. No science has defined, or can adequately define, him. Christian theology has only one statement to make about him: that he is a being created by Supreme Being, open to Supreme Being, in need of Supreme Being, in partnership and sonship with Supreme Being, and like Supreme Being itself, incomprehensible.

But canon law, a man-made codex, says quite the opposite about him.

Canon law says that this incomprehensible creature can be understood and judged by the rules of human evidence.

Canon law says that this mysterious oneness can be split, so that it is one thing in law and another in fact.

The Church teaches that man is the subject and the object of salvation: saving, safekeeping for his ultimate union with Supreme Being. At the same time canon law often denies him the means of his safekeeping: love, mutual support, a necessary support against that solitude which is a foretaste of damnation.

Canon law says that a defective man may not use even those faculties which he has to achieve a union of love with another willing creature.

Canon law sets the Assembly above the men without whom the Assembly would not exist. It sets an institution, the bond, above those for whose safekeeping the bond was made.

Canon law creates a fiction, the legal man, and sets him above existential man who is the authentic Son of God.

Canon law ignores that man is open, mobile, developing; instead it regulates and judges him by norms that are immobile, definitions that are static and criteria that degrade his mysterious, God-given dignity.

2. *The presumptions of canon law are all loaded against man for whose service and salvation the law is made.*

Canon law presumes an adequate knowledge of the essential quality of the marriage contract by both parties.

The presumption may be right. It may, with equal possibility, be wrong. Experience shows us every day that even intelligent people have enormous gaps in understanding, that the same verbalisms carry vastly different subjective connotations. Two men who recite the same creed or the same formula of contract may interpret the terms in a contrary sense. Language is at best an inadequate mode of communication.

The presumption is justified as a means of carrying on the normal commerce of human life, but it is not justified when it is intruded by statute into the moral life of the person, into the forum of his conscience where the law has no right of entry.

Only man knows what man knows. And even he is often unsure.

Canon law presumes a proper intention on the part of each spouse.

Again the presumption may be right or wrong. Again it is justified on pragmatic grounds. Again the balance of probability is too delicate to be loaded one way or the other. Ask us today what our intentions were yesterday and we will, perhaps, render them honestly, but we will certainly colour them without knowing it. Ask us ten years from now, and how can we answer at all? That which was buried in the subliminal consciousness has come to the surface. That which we thought we intended was not intended at all. That which we thought was not what we expressed in words.

Canon law presumes potency but does not define it clearly. As between man and woman it defines potency according to different norms.

This is bad law in any language.

Canon law makes physical impotence an invalidating impediment in marriage. It takes small and confused account of those psychic impotences which are much more common and which constitute much graver impediments to the physical and psychic union of marriage.

Sanity is presumed too. But sanity is nowhere defined in canon law, though the seeds of insanity of one kind or another may already be germinating before the marriage contract.

Free choice is presumed; but freedom is defined only by that which abrogates or impedes it. The indefinable limitations on freedom—the confusions of emotion, the subliminal fears, the nightmares that defy expression—these are non-accountable under the law.

The most unjust, the least justifiable presumption is that which lies at the root of all canonical procedures: that the discovery of truth, the arrival at absolute or at least moral certainty, is more important than the dispensation of justice to persons.

We submit that legal procedures—even the rigidly inquisitorial method of the canons—can rarely establish absolute certainty, that moral certainty is rare enough and that reasonable probability should be the norm of favourable judgment.

To require more than this, to prolong proceedings for the sake of absolute or moral certainty, is to inflict injustice.

3. *The favour of the bond over the persons is unjustified and unjustifiable.*

Attempts have been made by Catholic apologists to justify this legal norm on the grounds that it contributes to public order or alternately to maintain the sanctity of the bond.

We reject both the apologies. We maintain that the bond is sacred, precisely because it was made for a sacred person, man, his security and his salvation. Man forges the bond himself. The bond does not make man; man makes it, forges it for himself, because it corresponds with his mysterious nature, his openness and his need and his partnership in creation and procreation with Supreme Being.

If favour is to be granted, it can only be given to man.

Public order? This is a fiction based upon a fear of disorder which is a reality. To deny a right or a presumptive right to man for fear of a possible disorder in society is a craven act.

Fiat justitia et ruat coelum! Let justice be done and let the heavens fall! But they will not fall. And if the justice is only approximate, it is still better than no justice at all.

4. *The Church affects to offer a justice which it cannot and does not dispense.*

This is a grave charge and we know it. We submit we have proved it to the hilt.

The Church compels petitioners to seek justice at tribunals which have neither the time nor the staff to handle their cases.

She maintains in these tribunals archaic and inefficient procedures, which delay decision for years.

She imposes methods of mental and physical inquisition which are derogatory of human dignity.

She loads every norm and every procedure in favour of the bond and not the person.

She submits even a successful petitioner to double jeopardy by a mandatory appeal in favour of the bond.

She excludes from her judiciary the only people who have firsthand experience of the married state—married laymen and women.

She makes exorbitant and usurious demands on the patience and moral endurance of her children, to cover her own patent malfeasances.

When her children's patience runs out and they seek other remedies at other tribunals, she loads them with sanctions, and stigmas, and refuses them even the traditional tolerance of Christianity.

Justice delayed is justice denied. To promise justice when it cannot be delivered is a blatant hypocrisy. But to compel a man to an impossible recourse, and then sanction him when

for sheer survival he makes an accommodation between conscience and unavoidable circumstance—this surely is the most
monstrous injustice of all!

This is our case. This is our plea to the Assembly. "Refute
or reform. In God's name—let justice be done!"

BOOK 2

A PROPOSAL FOR REFORMS

Based upon
Christian concepts of the human
person, of the marriage relationship,
of the saving mission and the
legislating authority of the
Christian Assembly.

14
PRE–CONDITIONS FOR THE PROPOSALS

We need reform. We need it now. We are realists enough to know that we are not going to get it—at least in today's climate—on terms that lead to doctrinal disputes or involve the Church in a real or apparent retreat from her moral—or political—entrenchments.

So we laid down certain criteria for our proposals:

1. *That the proposed reforms should save the present official teaching of the Church on Christian marriage.*

This does not commit the writers to the position that the present official teaching is beyond discussion. It says that a revision of present official teaching is not required by their proposals.

2. *That the proposed reforms should not require the Church to restore the practice of divorce in the Church.*

There is strong evidence that she could. There is strong opinion that she should. We say categorically that she will not, in the immediate future. Given the unholy mess of her present tribunals, we think it is much better that she does not!

3. *That the proposed reforms should provide a speedy discharge for cases already in the machinery.*

Obviously there should not be two official systems of justice producing opposite consequences for marriage petitioners.

4. *That the proposed reforms should get the Church out of her present legal practice as soon as possible.*

We do not contest her right to engage in legal practice as a society. We say that prudence and the low standard of her present performance dictate a radical revision of her methods.

If our proposals meet these criteria—and we believe most firmly that they do—then a clear logic emerges. The Assembly has the means as well as the moral duty to remedy a patent and scandalous injustice.

15
THE PURPOSE OF REFORM

The end of all reform in this matter is to find, within the Deposit of Faith, an answer for those suffering people for whom a marital union has become intolerable. We believe that the answer exists, has always existed and has been obscured for too long. We believe that it can be applied without any legal acrobatics or legal fictions—and always with Christian justice, charity and compassion.

We have used the words Deposit of Faith with deliberate intent in this context.

The Deposit of Faith is a term which describes that whole body of truth which is available to all men for the proper conduct of their lives and their ultimate salvation.

The Deposit of Faith encompasses all truths, those made available by experience, by reason, by intuition, by human tradition, by Divine Revelation.

The Deposit of Faith is a corpus, a body, a oneness, as man is a oneness and God is a oneness. To ignore or disprize or lay false emphasis on any part of this corpus puts man in peril. To attempt to disjoin its parts by partisan selection is to court disaster.

Understand exactly what we are saying here. It is vitally important. All knowledge is one knowledge, because its object is a unified creation, the issue of a single creative act by Essential Unity. Therefore one truth never contradicts another, however difficult it may be to grasp the relationship between them. Therefore a phenomenon cannot be reasoned out of existence by sophistry or casuistry.

Let us be blunt and particular. An exegetist who tries to make a Biblical text fit a preconceived idea is committing a malfeasance. His charge is to examine the text in its historical and linguistic context and connotation, and to deliver a scholarly conclusion on its meaning. He cannot double in brass as a propagandist!

A historian who does not like what he finds in the history of the Church has no right to conceal or gloss the facts. He may offer an interpretation based on sound scholarship. But he must not offer the interpretation as history. A partisan interpreter does himself no credit and the truth no service.

A theologian who wrenches a phenomenon out of its existential context to make it fit a doctrinal formula is immediately in error. A phenomenal fact and a transcendental truth are parts of the same oneness. If their concordance is not immediately apparent, it is our apprehension which is at fault, or the formula which is incomplete.

In the same manner, a legislator who loads the law with fictions makes a cloak for his own incapacity. When he invests these fictions with an authority they do not merit, he does violence to truth. When he imposes sanctions to protect the authority, he brings the authority into disrepute.

To sum up: It is to the Deposit that our assent of faith is given. Whoever or whatever disjoins the Deposit is false to the Deposit.

16
THE BASE OF
REFORM—TRUTH

On the basis of universal human experience we hold these things to be true and, as true, contained in the Deposit:

> A man is a creature, open, needy and developing.
> A woman is a creature, open, needy and developing.
> Marriage between a man and a woman is an affirmation of their mutual needs. It is a means to supply those needs, and to promote their mutual development, in accordance with their existential natures.
> Marriage is not simply a contract. It is a condition of life entered into by a contract.
> Marriage is not simply an institution. It is a condition of life recognized as having an institutional character in the social order, because it corresponds with the needs of man and woman as they are.

On the basis of Revelation we hold these things to be true and, as true, contained in the Deposit:

> A man is a creature of Divine origin, ordered to a Divine destiny: union with the Source of Being.
> A woman is a creature of Divine origin, ordered to the same Divine destiny.
> Human marriage, therefore, as a state natural to man, is of Divine origin and ordering.

It is clear that there is no conflict between the two sets of propositions.

Revelation simply supplies two terms missing from the experiential truths: an origin for man, woman and their union; an end to which they are directed.

In other words, Revelation affirms that men and women have a nature which transcends their visible circumstance. But observable man is the common term on which believer and unbeliever can and, in general, do agree.

There are terms of agreement, too, on the nature of the marital union.

It is entered by mutual consent (contract). It is directed toward mutual development. The development implies an end: the safekeeping of the persons by mutual comfort and support, the safekeeping of the race by ensuring its perpetuation. Revelation does not deny this end, but extends it to the ultimate union of the saved or perfected couple with God.

Reason and Revelation both concur that if, because of insuperable impediments, the development is not possible, then the end is not achievable and the union is without meaning—invalid. In this case the contract is pointless. Therefore, metaphorically it is torn up and society records the fact.

On the basis of the Christian Revelation we hold these things to be true and, as true, contained in the Deposit:

> Through, in, and by the Christian Revelation, God, the Supreme Being, acts upon man and with man.
>
> When man accepts to remain open to God's disposal and to act, freely, in concert with his Creator, then he becomes a Christian.
>
> He is required to affirm his acceptance and consent by a public, symbolic, and efficacious act, the purifying rite of baptism.
>
> He is then a new person, in the sense that his relationship with the Creator has been perfected by a free gift from God and his own free consent in love.

The marriage of a man and woman who stand, each, in this
same relationship to the Creator, is a Christian marriage.

Christian marriage is still a human marriage. It is initiated
by consent, it is directed to the development and completion
of the human person. It is not observably different from other
human marriages. It is, however, transcendentally different
because of the perfected relationship of the parties with their
Creator and with each other.

It is because of this perfected relationship that the marriage
is indissoluble.

Again, let us be clear on the nature of our affirmation.

We are saying that Christian marriage is not made indissoluble by law. It is indissoluble by the nature of the relationship of the parties with one another and by their perfected relationship in and through Christ with the Creator.

On the other hand, we maintain, in complete conformity
with the Deposit, that what appears to be a Christian marriage
may not be so in fact; because the perfected relationship on
which it was presumed to be based did not exist in the first
place or could never come into existence because of insuperable defects in the persons themselves.

We maintain further that the total breakdown of a presump-
tively Christian marriage provides equally strong presumptive
evidence that the essential elements—a capacity for development and completion within the bond—were absent from the
beginning.

At present the Church enforces only one legal presumption:
the existence of the perfected Christian relationship. She admits the opposite presumption. She admits that an incapacity
for development and completion within the bond invalidates it;
but she defines the incapacity by such restricted criteria that
she produces the legal lunacy of a non-human man.

We submit that these criteria should be abolished and that
a more sane and tolerable one should be established in law. We

suggest that it should acknowledge the following propositions:

Man is by nature indefinable.

His relations with his fellows and with his Creator are similarly indefinable.

Human evidence can rarely establish absolute or even moral certainties about these relationships as they exist. Still less can it establish, with any degree of certainty, the state of mind, the innermost convictions, or the capacities of any human being. It cannot disjoin by any valid definition the past and the present of any given individual.

Therefore, since each man is the particular object of salvation and the object of the infinite mercy of God, every presumption that can be exercised in favour of man, in favour of his integrity, dignity and welfare as a human being, a child of God, is not only permitted but required to be exercised.

17
THE ARGUMENT FOR
THE NEW CRITERION

The argument begins with the fact that man is a developing creature. He is changeable and changing. His circumstances are changing, too—more rapidly than at any other period in history. His adaptive mechanism, physical and psychic, is being subjected to enormous stresses and strains.

Modern man lives often on the edge of madness, in a world that has spun out of his personal control. The casualties of contemporary society are legion. The list of their maladies is terrifying: physical breakdown, mental illness, narcotic addiction, anti-social hostility, anti-social fugue and emotional impotence.

If man is to survive at all, society has to provide—and still fails to provide—sufficient tolerances to enable this changing creature to adjust to change. Christian society—if it is what it claims to be—should provide more tolerances than any other. Demonstrably it does not; but it can and must.

It is a principle of moral judgment that the character of an act is determined not only by the act itself but by the disposition of him who performs it. Imputability in law and in morals should be determined by all the personal peculiarities of the subject-at-law. In other words, a morally sound legal code must seek to give each man a justice that fits his unique personal constitution. Insofar as it fails to do this, it fails of its purpose.

It seems a folly to labour this point. But the fact is that ideal law, like ideal man, is a fiction.

Every lawgiver tries to provide for too many things at once: to deliver justice, to punish delinquency, to maintain predetermined patterns of social behaviour, to protect against dissimulation and conspiracy, to uphold a political system, to satisfy the majority voter.

The Roman Catholic Church, like every other lawmaking society, has fallen victim to this diversity of intent. It is, however, less excusable than other societies, because it claims absolute power to legislate on absolute principles in the domain of morals and faith and social life.

So let's get back to principles!

The fact that a marriage has broken down completely determines a reasonable possibility, which may be determined into a reasonable probability, that the parties lacked the capacity to fulfill the contract in the first place.

There is nothing revolutionary in this. It is in line with all human experience.

The presumption is even stronger in today's society, where immature marriages are very common, and where the conditioning of young people by mass media may leave them, for a long time, fundamentally ignorant of the nature and obligations of Christian marriage.

They say they know, but in fact they do not know. They consent to that which they do not know. Or their consent is reserved to concepts of marriage which are fundamentally un-Christian. Their emotional confusion may be an impossible impediment to that whole union of the whole person which is of the essential nature of Christian marriage.

On the other hand, it is a matter of daily experience that second unions—some of them at face value illegal—do produce all the phenomena of a stable Christian marriage: love, mutual care, the promise of development and completion, a Christian upbringing for children. Since phenomena do not contradict truth, it is obvious that the existing canons determine human relationships too narrowly.

Knowledge is now determined by a simple affirmation that knowledge is possessed. Consent is determined by a form of consent. Capacity is determined only as a capacity to perform a single physical act, common to man and beast. The continuity of man as a developing person is denied by refusing to relate his post-marital to his pre-marital conduct, for example in the case of problems of sexual deviation. Similarly the fact of Christian baptism is not enough to establish the fact that a Christian marriage exists. All that it can determine is that two baptized persons have gone through a form of Christian marriage. After that presumption begins.

In the preparation of this book we have talked with hundreds of pastors and dozens of priests directly involved with marital cases. All of them have deposed, willingly or under pressure, in approximately the same terms:

> We have many cases in which we know, as certainly as any man can know, that the marriage is invalid. We can do nothing, because we must apply the norms of existing law and not the norms of daily experience.

We quote the words of a noble bishop spoken to us on an aircraft between London and New York:

> If I could exercise in law the same discretion about motives and states of mind which I exercise in the confessional, I could wipe half the marriage cases off my books overnight! I do not do it because I am a public person in the Church; because I am subject to surveillance and sanction by Rome; because I am afraid of creating a public scandal of disobedience to the law. But, believe me, I am in as great a dilemma of conscience as any of the petitioners in my court.

We wonder still which should be the determining factor: the danger of scandal, or the danger of destroying a man or a woman?

18
THE METHOD OF
DETERMINATION

We do not suggest that any presumption should be exercised without a preliminary determination. We acknowledge that it cannot be made lightly or without reference to evidential facts and to the claims of conflicting parties.

We do, however, assert that the methods of determination should be humane and consonant with human dignity; that they should be speedy, tolerant and visibly just; and that they should remove the Church forever from the shabby intolerances of courtroom and secret inquisition.

How can this be done? We propose as follows:

1. *Abolish altogether the existing diocesan courts and the Holy Roman Rota.*

The way they function at present is a scandal. They cannot be made to function better, because of the shortage of trained clerical staff. Their antiquated procedures impede justice and create injustice. Their inquisitorial methods are alien and often incomprehensible to the non-Latin world, whose petitioners therefore plead at a gross disadvantage.

Most important of all, they cannot adjudicate the internal forum, yet their decisions—or non-decisions—reach intimately into it.

2. *Abolish all mandatory referral to Rome.*

The facts divorced from the persons are not truly judicable. Persons divorced from their circumstances are not judicable either. No man should be judged in absentia. No judge in the world is competent to try a marriage case from a sheaf of type-script—and still less from a translation! And Roman law, both civil and ecclesiastical, is a cumbersome code full of out-dated concepts of the human person.

3. *Abolish immediately* favor matrimonii.

This would enable a large number of cases presently before the courts to be discharged in favour of petitioners who have waited already far too long.

Nothing in all this is new. None of it does violence to Christian tradition or Christian doctrine. It expresses opinion current at all levels of the Church today. On the contrary, it affirms pastoral authority and conduces to a speedy and visible justice enlightened by the fraternal charity of the whole Christian Assembly. Finally it provides a method by which a Christian can, in good conscience, adapt himself to existence in a plural world of which he is, willy-nilly, a citizen.

The only objection that can be raised—and it is hypothesis and not a proven fact—is that such a system would contribute to laxity and lack of respect for the bond of marriage. Our answer is this. Those who don't respect the bond don't respect it under any system. The present system contributes to laxity because petitioners in good faith are denied and know they are denied the justice they seek. There will always be delinquents and outlaws. But a law which creates delinquency is radically bad.

4. *Establish a primary discretion for the confessor in obvious cases.*

This discretion is now exercised by many confessors, but it is exercised illegally. It constitutes what one writer has called "tolerance by dissimulation." The need for dissimulation could and should be removed.

We submit that there is no need to boggle over what constitutes an obvious case. The most cautious parish priest has a casebook full of tragedies which one compassionate adjudication could solve.

5. *Establish in every diocese one or more pastoral groups with authority to hear doubtful or disputed cases and recommend a decision to the bishop for his ratification.*

These groups should consist of clergy and married Christian laity competent in medicine, law and domestic relations.

They could discharge a double function in counsel and mediation to restore unstable unions and an application of Christian and commonsense norms to the determination of the validity or non-validity of the bond.

Acting in this matter, they would preserve the authority of the Church on Christian marriage and yet demonstrate visibly the working of Christian justice and Christian charity in marital issues. Through this the collective mind of the Church could be expressed. Their collective experience could, in the long run, clarify many obscure areas of Christian life and point the way to more enlightened practice in the future.

6. *Proceed to an immediate revision of canon law in respect of marriage.*

The revision should be immediate. The present law makes defectors of men and women of good will. They know they have only one life to live, and they are desperate to live it with at least a minimum of dignity and a minimum of contentment.

The revision should be provisional and enacted with sufficient tolerances to adapt it to local conditions.

The revision should be made not only by clerical commissioners but by an expert international committee of married laity.

19
THE OBSTACLES
TO REFORM

There are many obstacles to reform. We acknowledge them
frankly. We will try to discuss them objectively. We list them
as follows:

1. *The number and diversity of people affected.*
There are more than five hundred million Roman Catholics
in the world. They live at different levels of social development, in a variety of culture patterns, under different political
systems.

They have all made some kind of local accommodation with
the law as it exists now, whether by local tolerances, by indifference, or by tacit or open rejection.

The Italians and the Spaniards have accommodated to the
prohibition of divorce by a system of socially acceptable concubinage. The Church contrives to live with the system and to
ignore the enormous injustice done to innocent partners and
to the children of irregular unions who can never be legit-
imized.

However, be it said that the proposed divorce law in Italy
has met with surprising opposition from many of the laity, not
only from those who are conscientiously opposed, but from
those who find the present system agreeable and don't want to
see it upset by a divorce system with alimony, maintenance,

property settlements and the rest.

In the plural societies of America, England and Northern Europe the pattern is very different, because the divorce system makes concubinage a difficult and often costly pastime for married people, and legitimacy for the child is considered a minimal justice to a new human being.

Among the poor of South America, where temporary unions are customary and carry no stigma, the law is irrelevant and the tacit tolerances exercised by the local clergy are very wide.

In the countries of the Eastern Rites, Greece, Yugoslavia, Lebanon, Syria and the rest, communicating Catholics feel that they have been deprived unjustly, by the Romans, of tolerances which were current in the East from the beginning and which their brethren of the Orthodox Churches continue to enjoy.

To devise reforms that will fit all these diverse situations is admittedly difficult.

One thing is very clear: the reforms cannot be accomplished by rigorism but only by enactments of Christian tolerance and compassion.

2. *The present centralism of the Roman Catholic Church.*

Let us be careful how we specify this obstacle.

The hierarchic order on which the Church is founded is traditional and fundamental. We accept it as such.

It is the manner in which this hierarchy functions at this moment which constitutes the obstacle.

Here is how the organization works in fact:

The Pope is its head, vested with enormous power. His instruments of government are the Sacred Congregations and other bodies, which constitute a central bureaucracy, located in Rome.

After these—not in rank, but in administrative order!—come the patriarchs, archbishops and bishops in whom regional authority is invested. Below the bishops are the pastors and the assisting priesthood. Last of all come the laity in their hundreds of millions!

The laity are the subjects, objects and, in this case, the victims of hierarchic legislation. They have no voice in making the laws, no appeal against them and no hand in framing changes for the future.

In spite of—and also because of—the vast powers vested in him, the Pope is isolated and infinitely vulnerable. To quote from another writing:

> The Papacy is the most paradoxical office in the world; the most absolute and yet the most limited; the richest in revenues but the poorest in personal return. It was founded by a Nazarene carpenter who owned no place to rest His head, yet it is surrounded by more pomp and panoply than is seemly in this hungry world. It owns no frontiers, yet is subject always to national intrigue and partisan pressure. The man who accepts it claims Divine guarantee against error, yet is less assured of salvation than the meanest of his subjects. The keys of the kingdom dangle at his belt, yet he can find himself locked out for ever from the Peace of Election and the Communion of Saints. If he says he is not tempted by autocracy and ambition, he is a liar. If he does not walk sometimes in terror, and pray often in darkness, then he is a fool.

It is not to be expected, therefore, that the man who is the reigning Pope can or will be always the initiator of needed reforms. Even if he initiates them, their execution can be stalled by the bureaucracy.

Reforms will not originate from the bureaucracy either. A bureaucracy, by its very nature, is conservative, administrative, concerned with the method and methodology of existing legislation.

A bishop can do much better—if he has light and compassion and great courage. A bishop's authority derives directly from the Apostles. It is collegial with the authority of the Pope.

A bishop stands in the same relation to the Pope as Paul did to Peter.

A pastor can do much—if he has tenacity and compassion. But he cannot legislate and he is vulnerable to censorship, surveillance and canonical sanctions.

The laity? They do not know what they can do. They have not yet been heard. Their silence is an enormous obstacle to action because the full mind of the full Church remains unspoken.

There is only one way in which the obstacle can be removed. The laity must organize themselves to present their grievances and their legitimate requirements to their bishops. They must organize widely, strongly, conjoining their various organizations throughout the world, so that their petitions cannot be buried in the archives of the bureaucracy or robbed of their urgency by diplomatic editing.

The hierarchy is a function of the Assembly and exists for the service of the Assembly. The whole Assembly must speak and its voice must be heard at the See of Peter.

3. *The bachelor psychosis within the Church.*

The writers did not coin this phrase. It was uttered by Patriarch Maximos IV at the Second Vatican Council.

We have adopted it to name what we consider a big obstacle to reform of the marriage laws: to wit, that the laws are, and will continue to be, framed by celibate clerics who may know the theory but certainly not the practice of marriage!

The Church very wisely appoints lay bankers to handle her money. Why has she never appointed to the judiciary of the Rota married men and women? Is she afraid of her own children?

Or does the bachelor psychosis lead inevitably to Byzantinism with all its unhealthy connotations of secrecy, eunuchry, the inflation of central authority, and a Manichean misprision of the oneness of man?

4. *Unreadiness to delegate authority within the Church.*

The authority of the Roman Catholic Assembly is vested in the reigning Pontiff as Vicar of Christ and Successor of Peter.

Anyone vested with authority may delegate it, in whole or part.

The delegation from the Pontiff to the Sacred Congregations is great. It has to be. But the delegation from the Congregations, where so much power is involved, is at best a grudging affair, hedged with reservations and referrals.

The tendency of every bureaucracy is to centralize, to perpetuate its functions and extend them. The clerical bureaucracy is as adept at this as any other. There is much talk of the struggle in the Church between conservatives and liberals. It would be more accurate to define it as a struggle between the centralizers who want to see more and more power vested in Rome and the local bishops who want a greater use of legitimate episcopal authority in local areas.

The decentralizers are at a disadvantage. Like the laity they are a long way from the seat of power. They can easily be damaged by rumour, critical comment and, sometimes, by slanderous report in Rome. But they do have power and they can use it to great effect if they have compassion and courage—and are prepared to do occasional bloody battle with the bureaucrats.

Those who have come best out of the battles to date are those who have the respect, affection and fraternal loyalty of their people, because the people have found them trusted interpreters of their needs!

There are historical factors at work here too. The Church has fought a long and losing battle to hold legislative power in civil society—on the evidence of history, it is well that she has lost the battle. Where she still holds influence by concordat, her political performance tends to be suspect. She is in the world and of it—too much of it for the comfort of a Christian conscience.

We have still to live down the memory of inquisitions and minority persecutions and Holy Empires and so-called Christian states! But even Christians misread the lessons of history!

5. *Static concepts of man and of marriage.*

Speculation has never been livelier in the Church than it is now. Clerical speech has never been freer. The inquisition is gone—almost! The Index doesn't exist. How then can we charge that static concepts are an obstacle to reform?

Because in the Church there is still a great gulf fixed between the theologian and the lawmaker. Opinion is not law, as the veterans of the Vatican well know. The law is what counts in the end, because the law is the ultimate instrument of power. And the law is still what it was before Vatican II, based on the same presumptions about the human person and the marriage relationship.

Official teaching is static, too, as we found on the contraception issue, and the liberal theologian, the forward-looking bishop have to hedge their utterances with careful qualifications lest their orthodoxy or their obedience be called in question.

Free speech is still not encouraged in the Church; criticism of persons or practice is perennially unwelcome. And though the Holy Office has another name now, it still takes a brave man to speak his mind publicly on the Doctrine of the Faith.

He can do it in speculative writing. He can raise any issue he likes in a theological commission—which is already a great gain! But in the pulpit, not yet, not now! We hungry sheep look up and are not fed.

In spite of all these obstacles we still believe that reforms can be accomplished, reforms in full conformity with sound doctrine, venerable practice and the demands of justice and charity.

We believe it because we believe that the Spirit of God is at work in the Assembly, whose discontents are a symptom of a

Divine dynamic towards renewal. The members of the Assembly protest because they care. They are restless because they hunger and thirst after justice.

When they fall silent and indifferent they are, at that moment, lost to the Assembly!

6. *The Roman concept of law and legality.*

This is, in our opinion, the biggest obstacle of all.

Get drunk in a London pub and hit a policeman; you will be charged with a misdemeanour. Get drunk in a Roman bar and hit a Roman policeman, you will be charged with an aggravated offense against the majesty of the state and you'll get up to three years in the pokey. The basic concept is different. A policeman in London is the servant of the people. In Italy the policeman is representative of the state, that mysterious entity which exists apart from the people.

Smoke hashish in London; you may be arrested, charged, released on bail and ultimately tried or given a suspended jail sentence. Do the same thing in Italy, you *will* be arrested, imprisoned without bail, held in confinement until the instructing judge either indicts you for later trial or releases you because he has not enough evidence to indict. If you are released, you will have no recourse for false arrest and you will be required to pay the state the cost of your maintenance during your unjust imprisonment. There is no habeas corpus! The state is paramount. The person is a subject.

The law of the Roman Catholic Church is Roman law, pure and undiluted by Anglo-Saxon or any other concepts. The law is conceived, framed and promulgated in Roman terms of reference—but the Roman tolerances are unwritten, unrecognized—and therefore difficult of access to the outsider.

Put it another way. In Anglo-Saxon law the tolerances are built into the law by statute. In Roman law they are applied in a non-statutory fashion before you get to law. Once you get to law, you've had it, little brother! The confrontation between the person and the state—or the Church!—under a Latin system is always disadvantageous to the person, because the state is by concept self-existent, self-justifying and obliged to self-justification.

This is why the centralized system of law and legal administration in the Church divides and will continue to divide the Assembly. This is why we need local episcopal autonomy, to apply a universal principle—the Faith—by local legal norms.

Unless and until we get it the Church will continue to be divided and will be more deeply divided in the future.

The principle of Christian conduct is not at stake. It is the Roman practice which obscures the principle. Man must be adjudicated as he is, where he is, by practices which he understands. The Lex Romana as a universal code is a dead letter which is killing the Faith of millions.

Does this sound like an exaggeration? We insist that it is not.

There are few reliable statistics, but, whichever way one computes the available or estimated figures, they run into many millions. And the problem is by its nature a continuing and increasing one. The discredit to the Church continues and will increase, unless reforms begin now. The defections of decent people and the loss of their families to the Christian Assembly will continue, too, unless they are offered a compassionate Christian solution to their dilemmas.

20
WHO IS ACCOUNTABLE?

Official lamentations about the breakdown of family life and the corruption of morals are no solution at all. Family life has always been unstable—if only by reason of recurrent wars and the great ground swells of human development. We have had two world wars in our generation. We have witnessed the enforced collectivization of hundreds of millions of people. The massive urbanization of industrial civilizations has brought a huge disruptive pressure to bear on social units.

But the existing legislation of the Church takes no account of cataclysms and contrives, dangerously, to justify its own stasis in a dynamic world.

The early lawgivers knew better than this. Even in the seventh century there was legislation permitting the remarriage of a spouse whose partner had been carried off by raiders and sold into slavery.

Let it not be claimed either that reforms must be slow because the revision of any codex takes a long, long time. This is a specious nonsense.

The Roman Pontiff has power to establish, by simple fiat, a vast delegation of authority to local bishops, and a humane norm of judgment which would override all the existing canons. The people know that he has this power. They hold him ultimately responsible for the injustice which is enacted under his authority. And his authority is thereby grievously damaged because it is vested in him for the service of the Servants of God, whoever they may be.

Yet the faithful are more compassionate to their Pontiff than he appears to be to them. They pity him for the burdens he carries, they recognize his age and his infirmities, they excuse him from personal guilt and presume the highest intentions even for his most vacillating performances. But their endurance and their patience are not infinite, and they wait—but will not all or always wait—for the Builder of Bridges to throw the first span across the river which separates too many believers from their brothers of the Assembly.

The administrators of the Church are accountable, too, not because they hold vast delegated power, but because they have the commission to inform and advise the Pontiff. Some of them do. Some of them do not. Some of them seem like courtiers who feel bound to praise every lightest word of the Prince as if it were a revelation from Thabor. Paul withstood Peter, the Vicar of Christ, when he tried to impose circumcision upon Gentile Christians. Likewise every member of the hierarchy and of the central administration has a duty to represent the needs of the Assembly, openly and vigorously to the Servant of the Servants of God.

Bishops are accountable, too, because they are the heads of local churches, they are the successors of the Apostles, they have the Apostolic autonomy and a collegiality with Peter. If they do not raise their voices for their own flocks—and many of them do not, and many more are not heard to do so!—then they are partakers in the manifest scandal we are now contending with.

Pastors are accountable if they lack the courage to plead and to contest for the souls entrusted to their care.

And the laity—the hundreds of millions of the Assembly? They too are accountable if they sit smug and silent while their unhappy brothers and sisters suffer under the burdens of intolerable law. They have a noble precedent to plead—a precedent which has been too long obscured and forgotten—the practice of the Church from earliest times. We expose it now in the ensuing chapters.

BOOK 3

THE TOLERANCES OF THE EARLY CHURCH

As expressed
in the writings of the early Fathers,
the legislation of the Synods and the
pronouncements of the Popes.

21
TOLERANCE—
WHAT IS IT?

Tolerance is a chameleon word. It can assume a whole gamut of colorations. It can suggest laxity, permissiveness, cynicism, indifference, amusement, a degree of contempt, an acceptable variation of norms. The sense in which we use it here is the more primitive one: the capacity to bear the burden of human frailty, to accommodate to it, to accept it without rancour and with a remedial intention.

Tolerance in this sense is an aspect of Christian charity. It is an affirmation of the familial nature of the Assembly, of the whole human household. "My little children, love one another! . . . carry one another's burdens!"

Tolerance signifies not only a passive endurance but an activity—a provision of means by which the burdens of existence may be eased. The Good Samaritan is Christ's prototype of the active carrier of other men's loads.

So when we talk of the tolerances of the early Church we are not talking of lax practices, of dubious compromises, but of active measures taken by the Assembly in other times to help its members to survive the tragedies of life and remain still Christ-directed and Christ-centered.

The tolerances of the early Church acknowledge at once the perfection of the Christian ideal and the imperfections of those who struggle to reach it. They require repentance and reformation, but they provide the means for both. They acknowledge "Divine Grace" for what it truly is—not a vague something discussed by theologians and casuists; but a gift of the means of saving, in, through and by the Christian Assembly, which Christ instituted to perpetuate His Own saving mission. When these tolerances are removed or denied, a portion of the Saving Gift is denied too. And in today's confused and confusing world, when the impact of every event is felt immediately on every human organism, we can ill afford the deprivation.

People are more aware of their "selfhood" than they ever were before. They know more about their bodily functions, more about the intricacies of their psyches, than their forefathers. As a consequence, they are more aware of the mystery of the self. The more they are aware of mystery, the less they are prepared to accept draconic solutions to the human dilemma or pat answers to the questions which plague them every hour.

A Papal Encyclical, written in the formal and sterile style of the courts, makes no impression on the poignantly involved self. A half-hour sermon on Sunday, didactic or hortatory, leaves the self still solitary. Ten minutes in the confessional for a ritual recital of faults, a ritual counselling, a ritual absolution, is small solace for a self haunted by the horrors of our time—tyranny and mass murder, and hunger, and the conspiracies of violence.

We are ourselves. We have begotten other selves. How do we survive, sane and human, in a madness of animals?

We selves are becoming more and more isolated in this century of the conglomerates. We have long since been detribalized. Now, in the great cities, we are being defamilialized— an ugly and artificial word for an ugly and unnatural situation. We live apart in boxes called apartments. We bore peepholes in the door to spy out hostile intruders. The capitalist economy forces us to be competitive. The socialized economy makes us rivals in a bureaucracy. The self is forced to become a function in the collective. The collective fears the self. The self, in fear or hatred of the collective, either withdraws into a foetal dark or explodes outward in a revolutionary crisis.

Either way the risks are enormous. The self-in-fugue has no point of arrival except a dark corner of a dark room, where it huddles, blind, deaf and dumb, paralyzed with fear of nameless horrors. The self-in-revolt fragments itself in anger, lust and violence until all the king's horses and all the king's men— and all the therapists in the world—cannot put it together again.

The risks to the self grow greater every day as new energies are released by scientific discovery and mass communication and geopolitical changes. The reaction against the risks grows stronger too. Violence creates conspiracy. Conspiracy begets fear and fragmentation. And the self-at-risk, for want of other fraternity, throws itself into the conflict. It is the terror of our times. We try to survive by destruction.

So when we attempt to reveal once more the tolerances of the early Church, it is to restudy their significance for our circumstances and to revitalize the charity and the compassion upon which they were founded. The magistracy of the Church we know. We hear it debated—God help us!—far too often and too loudly in our times. We wait still to see the full performance of her ministry—her service of love to the human family.

22
OF HISTORY AND HISTORIANS

Man is a natural myth-maker. Give him an unpleasant fact and
he will try to charm it out of existence by magic. If the magic
fails, he will try to protect himself against the unpleasantness
by turning it into a myth—as the oyster makes a pearl out of
a piece of shell grit. Of course the pearl is real, but the myth is
an illusion.

A good historian deals with recorded facts—pleasant or unpleasant. He must be objective and impartial. He must use all
available evidence. He must not invent evidence. He must not
suppress it. He may offer interpretation, but he must base the
interpretation on sound scholarship. He is not excluded from
guesswork. But he must not present a guess as a proven proposition. If he fails in any of these functions, he is relegated to
the ranks of the myth-makers, the propagandists, the political
pamphleteers, or the plain incompetents.

For this reason we are disposed to great caution in what we
write now. We read history, but we do not claim historical
scholarship. We acknowledge our debt to other scholars for
source materials and references. When we tender comments we
distinguish them as private opinions. We do not seek to endow
them with a fictitious authority.

This being said, we make a few simple distinctions. History
records both what happened and what contemporaries said

about the happenings. What they said contains exposition, description, commentary, criticism, exhortation—the expression of a variety of subjective attitudes to an historic fact.

What was done and what was said—sometimes what was unsaid too—establish the "climate of the period": an indicator to the way groups of people acted and thought at the time in question. "Climate," of course, is the sum of a number of variables and opposites, sunshine and storm, high pressure and low, cloud and clear sky; but it can and does express a prevailing pattern which is a kind of constant.

But one has to keep in mind that the variables produce the constant and that the opposites co-exist.

When an early theologian debated the practice of divorce, it was because divorce was practiced in his day. When bishops or Synods or Popes legislated for or against certain licenses, it was in view of existing situations.

The wisdom of their opinions, the moral rightness of their decisions, whether or no these decisions can or should apply in our times—these are outside the present question.

We are concerned here with the facts of Christian tradition. The facts are these: that, in the solution of marital problems, much greater tolerance was exercised in the early Church than is exercised today; that divorce was permitted, for a variety of reasons, in the Church; that remarriage of divorced persons was permitted; that divorce and remarriage were matters of canonical legislation in both East and West.

For proof we bring forward the witness of the Fathers, the Synods and the early Popes.

23
THE TESTIMONY OF THE FATHERS

According to Vincent of Lerins (fifth century) the Fathers of the Church are

> those writers of Christian antiquity who, each in his own time and place, were accredited teachers of the one faith in union with the Assembly.

The Encyclopaedia Britannica widens the definition a little:

> The Fathers of the Church are the great bishops and other eminent Christian teachers of the early centuries who were conspicuous for soundness of judgment and sanctity of life, and whose writings remained as a court of appeal for their successors especially in reference to controverted points of Faith or practice.

The Fathers, therefore, are respectable witnesses, to say the least! They were divided on many points, as Christians are divided today; but their credit as teachers was not thereby damaged, nor their communion with the Assembly broken. It is clear that they were often in dilemma, as we are. It is equally clear that they found themselves obliged to assert the practice of Christian common sense in the conduct of tangled human lives.

Tertullian (+ 247) was one of the greatest Christian writers of his day. It was he who coined the phrase: "The blood of martyrs is the seed of the Church." In later life he joined the rigorist sect of the Montanists who forbade, among other things, second marriages. Tertullian makes three statements, of which the third contradicts the other two.

In his "Treatise against Marcion" he says bluntly:

Even Christ defended the rightness of divorce.
[Habet itaque et Christum assertorem iustitia divortii.]

In his "Letter to the Wife" he writes:

Now, with reference to human frailty, let us speak of another kind of conduct. We are compelled to do this by the example of certain women, who having been offered the *opportunity* of practicing continence by reason of *divorce* or the death of the husband not only rejected the opportunity of such a perfect life, but *in remarrying were not even mindful of the rule that they should marry in the Lord.*

Later when he joined the Montanist sect he prescribed more harshly:

We are not allowed even to marry, although we put our wives away.

Origen of Alexandria (183–254) was even closer to Apostolic times and provides an encyclopedia of information on the mind of the early Church. He wrote in Greek. He studied and taught in Alexandria, Rome, Arabia and Palestine. He was imprisoned and tortured in the persecution of Decius but survived to die in liberty. His reputation for chastity and severity of life gave rise to a malicious legend that he had castrated himself.

In his "Testimony to Quirinus" he affirms the practice of divorce, disagrees with it and offers a mitigating explanation:

Even now, here acting outside of holy Scripture, some su-
periors of the Church have permitted to a woman to marry
while her husband is alive . . . *Yet, they did not act without reason because, so is seems, they have accorded condescension outside of what had been prescribed and trans-
mitted in order to prevent worse consequences.*

Lactantius Firmiancus (circa 250–330) was a teacher of
rhetoric, born in Africa. He became a convert to Christianity
and in old age became the tutor to Crispus, the son of the Em-
peror Constantine I. In his Epitome, *Divinarum Institutionum*
he wrote:

However, as the wife is constrained by the obligation of chastity not to desire another man, so also the man is held to the
same law, because God has joined man and wife in the bond
of one only body. *He commanded, therefore, not to dismiss
a wife except if proven guilty of adultery, and that the bond
of the conjugal contract never be dissolved except that which
perfidy has broken.*

St. Basil of Cappadocia (330–379) is universally regarded
as one of the great teachers of the Church. Between 344 and
375 he wrote a number of letters to Amphilochius, Bishop of
Iconium. These letters were later divided into eighty-five "canons." Many of these deal with marriage discipline in the
Church. They are clear evidence of a respected discipline dif-
fering greatly from that which exists today.

They give even clearer testimony to the character of Basil
himself, humane, tolerant, a respecter of decent custom, passionately orthodox, but never fanatical.

While reading the following extracts from the canons, it is
important to remember the distinctions which were made in
Roman law and Church law at this time.

Adultery was the offense committed with a married woman
by a man, married or unmarried.

A married man who slept with an unmarried woman committed only fornication.

A husband might divorce his wife for adultery. A wife had no recourse against even an adulterous husband.

Canon 9. *The declaration of the Lord, that it is not permitted to separate a marriage except for the cause of fornication, applies equally to men as to women, if one considers the logical consequences of the idea. However, the custom is different, and we find many more demands imposed upon women.*

Canon 9 (cont.). . . . . But the custom also orders adulterous man and those who are in the state of fornicators not ·to forsake their wives. *This is why, if one of these was abandoned (by his spouse), I do not say that one can treat as an adulteress the woman who afterwards marries him.*

Canon 9 (cont.). . . . . *As to the husband who was abandoned, it can be excused (if he remarries), and the woman who lives with him under such conditions is not condemned. Nevertheless, if the man himself has abandoned his (innocent) wife, and if he has joined up with another, then he himself is an adulterer, because he has made his legitimate wife commit adultery; and she who cohabits with him is also adulterous because she attracted the husband of another woman.*

The following canons may come as a shock to many of today's Catholics. The first indicates a very tolerant approach to non-marital unions, and the second indicates that illegal remarriages receive a condonation by lapse of time and by appropriate penance.

Canon 26. Fornication is not marriage; it is not even the beginning of marriage. That is why, if it is possible to induce to separate those who have united themselves in fornication, this is the best thing to do. *But if they absolutely desire to live together, the penance reserved for fornication shall be imposed upon them, yet without separating them, lest something worse should result.*

Canon 77. He who has deserted a woman with whom he was lawfully united in order to take another is certainly subject to condemnation as an adulterer in virtue of the sentence of the Lord; *but it was decided by our Fathers that the culpable ones shall do penance as weepers for one year, that they shall be hearers two years, and prostrati three years; that the seventh year they shall stand with the faithful, and they shall be judged worthy of the offering if they have done penance with tears.*

St. Asterius (d. c.400) was Bishop of Amasya in Asia Minor. He was a noted preacher in his day and twenty-one of his sermons are still extant. He preached clearly that only death and adultery dissolved a marriage:

This you should hold as established and be entirely persuaded of, that marriage can be dissolved for no cause whatever, except because of death and adultery.

St. Epiphanius of Salamis (310–403) was a native of Palestine. He became abbot at Eleutheropolis where he wrote and preached against the Arian heresy and was acclaimed "the oracle of Palestine." He was made Archbishop of Salamis in Cyprus in 367. His most compendious work is the *Panarion* (a remedy against heresies). In this work he states:

He who cannot keep continence after the death of his first wife, or who has separated from his wife for a valid motive, as fornication, adultery, or another misdeed, if he takes another wife, or if the wife takes another husband, the Divine word does not condemn him nor exclude him from the Church or the life; but she tolerates it rather on account of his weakness. Not that this man can keep with him two wives, the first one still gravitating around him; but if he is actually separated from his first wife, he may take another according to the law, if this is his desire.

St. Chromatius of Aquileia was a correspondent of St. Jerome, St. Ambrose and other notable contemporaries. Seventeen of his treatises survive, all of them on the Gospel of St. Matthew.

Except on account of adultery, it is not permitted to dismiss a wife; thereby clearly establishing that he acts against the will of God who recklessly presumes to separate by an illicit divorce a marriage joined together by God . . .

However, as it is not lawful to dismiss a wife leading a chaste and pure life, so it is also permitted to dismiss an adulterous woman, because she has rendered herself unworthy of her husband's companionship, he who by sinning with her body has dared to violate the temple of God.

St. Cyril of Alexandria (376–444) was Patriarch of Alexandria and presided at the Council of Ephesus in 431. Leo XIII declared him a Doctor of the Church.

Cyril declares categorically that adultery dissolves the marriage bond and adds a rider. "God, as I firmly believe, adapted his laws to the measure of human nature."

On the other hand, he writes in deprecation of remarriage after divorce:

By dismissing the wife he gives her an opportunity to remarry, which is a kind of adultery, similar to a bond that is not yet dissolved.

St. Augustine of Hippo (354–430) is the strongest and most arbitrary of the early Fathers in defense of the absolute indissolubility of marriage. It is his thought more than any other which colours the present official teaching of the Church. However, even St. Augustine adverts to the contrary practice as subsisting in his day:

However, how can it be *that the husband is permitted to marry another woman after he had repudiated an adulterous wife,* while the wife is not [permitted] to marry another man after she has left an adulterous husband, I cannot see . . .

St. Theodore of Canterbury (602–690) was born in Tarsus. He is commonly called the second founder of Canterbury and the first primate of the English Church. It was he who called the first National Council of the English Church at Hereford in 673. His surviving writings are contained in a document called "The Penitential of Theodore," which consists of his decisions in disciplinary matters. Here are some of the decisions:

XIII.5. If a slaveman or a slavewoman have been joined in matrimony by the master of both, and later the slaveman, or the slavewoman, has become free, if he or she who remains in slavery cannot be bought free, *the free spouse is permitted to marry a free person.*

31. To him whose wife has been taken away by the enemy, if he cannot retrieve her, *it is permitted to take another wife; it is better to do this than to commit fornication.* And if she returns later, he is not obliged to receive her back if he has another. *She herself may take another husband if she had only one before.*

61. If the wife was taken away into captivity by force, *he can take another wife after one year.*

140. *The layman whose wife left him can, with the consent of the bishop, take another after two years.*

24. If that wife again returns to him afterwards, he is not obliged to receive her back if she had another man, but she can take another husband if she had only one before. The same rule applies to slaves from overseas.

20. If a wife that was abducted by force into captivity cannot be redeemed, he may take another after one year.

21. Likewise, if she was taken into captivity, the husband shall wait five years, and similarly the wife, if this should happen to the husband.

22. If, therefore, the husband took another wife, he shall take back the former wife if she returns from captivity, and the second one he shall dismiss; likewise, she shall do as we said above, if this should happen to the husband.

19. *If a wife left her husband out of disrespect for him, and refuses to return and be reconciled with the husband, it will be permitted to him to take, with the consent of the bishop, another wife after five years.*

143. If somebody's wife has committed fornication, it is permitted to dismiss her and to take another.

II.5. #5. If the wife of anyone commits fornication, it is allowed to dismiss her and to take another; that is, if the husband dismisses his wife because of fornication, and she was his first wife, he is permitted to take another wife; *while she, if she agrees to do penance for her sins, may take another man after five years.*

We would quote much more extensively from the early Fathers, but some of the available material would involve us in a historical exegesis and a debate on conflicting interpretations which we do not feel competent to undertake.

However, we submit the witness is clear. Divorce and remarriage were permitted and legislated in patristic times.

We feel justified, too, in adding a personal comment.

Whatever the conflict of opinion, it is clear that learned and holy men did apply in their marriage judgments two fundamental principles of Christian theology: the principle of economy—which requires that *imperfect* man must co-operate to the best of his ability to realize the ideal proposed to him in Christ; the principle of equity—which dictates that no law should be applied in a manner disproportionate to the end which the law has in view—in this case the saving of the human person.

24
THE TESTIMONY OF THE SYNODS

The Synods of the Church provide an important testimony, because they enacted legislation and thus gave a canonical form to local or regional practice. The witness of the Synods is especially interesting because it shows that completely contrary laws were enacted on the same subject at different times and in different places, but by bishops in communion with the same Apostolic Church.

The Council of Arles (314) issued twenty-two enactments. This is one of them:

> Canon 10. To those who apprehend their wives in adultery, who are young believers and not prohibited from marrying, it is agreed [placuit] that, as far as possible, *counsel should be given* not to take other wives in spite of the fact that the living wives are adulterous.

A seventeenth-century edition of the Acts of this Council quotes St. Augustine on this decision:

> The Fathers of this very renowned council do not inflict any punishment but give only a counsel. Thus, the Fathers say that the matter is not forbidden.

The Council of Vannes (461 or 465) ruled as follows:

Canon 2. In respect also of those who have deserted their wives, as it is said in the Gospel "except for fornication," and have without proving adultery married others, we decree that they are likewise to be barred from communion, lest the sins passed over by our indulgence should attract others to the licentiousness of error.

The Council of Agde (506) was held under the presidency of St. Caesarius of Arles. Among other things it treated of marriage dissolutions:

However, those laymen who dissolve married life or have already dissolved it, committing a serious sin, and do not furnish any probable reasons for the separation, dissolving for this reason their marriages in order to attempt unlawful or forbidden ones—if they, before having submitted the ground for separation to the provincial bishops and before the wives have been found guilty by the court, had driven them away, then such husbands shall be excluded from the ecclesiastical communion and from the holy assembly of the people, because they defile faith and marriage.

The Synod of Hereford (673) testifies the current practice in England:

Every priest shall publicly admonish the people to abstain from unlawful marriages, for a lawful marriage can by no means be separated in accordance with the command of the Lord, *except by reason of fornication, or except by mutual consent and this because of the service of God.*

The Council of Soissons (744) limited the grounds of divorce and remarriage to adultery on the part of the wife:

Canon 9. Similarly, we decree that no layman shall take as wife a woman consecrated to God, nor a relative of his, nor shall during the lifetime of a husband another man take his wife, nor shall the wife during the lifetime of her husband take another man, *because the husband must not dismiss his woman except because he apprehended her in fornication.*

The Council of Verberie (752) made more sweeping enactments and legislated for causes of divorce and remarriage other than adultery:

Canon 2. If anyone stays with his step-daughter, he cannot have either the mother or her daughter, nor can he nor she at any time marry anybody else. The wife, however, if she so wishes, and if she cannot be continent, after she has found out that her daughter was in adultery with the husband shall not have carnal intercourse with him, *and if she does not wish to abstain voluntarily, can marry another.*

Canon 5. If a wife seeks in conspiracy with others to procure the death of her husband and her husband killed the man in defending himself, and he can prove this, *this husband, as it appears to us, can dismiss the wife, and if he wishes take another.* The ambushing wife herself shall be subjected to penance and shall remain without hope of marriage.

Canon 9. If a man, compelled by unavoidable necessity, has fled to another duchy or province, or if he had followed his lord, to whom he had promised faith and faithfulness and therefore cannot refuse, and his wife, although she could and is able, will not go with him because of her love for her parents or relatives, she shall forever stay unmarried as long as the husband whom she did not follow lives. *But he who remains in another country because of a compelling need, if he has no hope of ever returning to his home country, and if he cannot live continently, may take another wife, after having done penance.*

Canon 10. If the son slept with his step-mother, the wife of his father, neither he [the son] nor she can attain marriage. *But that man [the father], if he wishes, can have another wife; but it is better to abstain.*

Canon 11. If anyone slept with his step-daughter, he can be subject to the same sentence; and with the sister of his wife, he can be treated in the same way.

Canon 18. He who stays with a cousin of his wife shall be deprived of his own wife, and shall not have any other; that woman whom he had may do what she wishes. This the Church does not accept.

Canon 21. He who permitted his wife to accept the veil may not accept another wife.

A Council at Rome during the reign of Pope Stephen II (752–757) delivered this enactment:

Canon 36. Nobody is permitted, except on the ground of fornication, to abandon a wife with whom he had intercourse and then to marry another; if it happened otherwise, it is proper that the transgressor rejoin the first marriage. If, however, the man and the wife agree among themselves that they would separate only for the sake of entering religious life, this shall not be done without the knowledge of the bishop, in order that they may be questioned each in a determined place. For if the wife or husband is opposed the marriage is not dissolved for such a cause.

A Council of sixty-two bishops held at Rome in 826 during the reign of Pope Eugene II promulgated this same Canon 36 in the same form.

The Synod of Pope Leo IV held in Rome in 853 promulgated the same canons again. The interesting point is that these canons which permitted divorce and remarriage were enacted *in Rome after* the rigorist pronouncement of Compiègne, Friuli and Paris to which we point now.

The Council of Compiègne (757) passed the Canon 13 permitting one partner to enter religious life with the consent of the other and allowing to other partner to remarry. It appended a note to this canon that the Papal Legate, George, Bishop of Ostia, had agreed to it.

It made other liberal legislation as well:

Canon 6. A Frank accepted from his lord a fief in another province, and he took with him his vassal. When then later the lord died, the aforementioned vassal continued to stay there. Another man accepted then the same fief, and in order to secure the service of the same vassal, he gave him a wife from the same fief, and he had her for a certain time. But since this lord mistreated him, he dismissed the wife and returned to the family of his late lord, and took another wife. *It was decided that he may have her whom he took later.*

Canon 8. If a man has a legitimate wife and his brother commits adultery with her, that brother and that woman who committed adultery shall never have [a right to] marriage. *He whose wife she was, if he wishes, is entitled to take another wife.*

The Council of Friuli (791) ruled, however, in the most rigorous terms against divorce for any reason at all:

Chapter 10. Likewise, it pleased [to decree] that it shall not be permitted to the husband, the matrimonial bond having been dissolved because of fornication, to take another wife as long as the adulterous spouse is alive, despite the fact that she is adulterous . . . Therefore, one is given patently to understand: the husband is not permitted, nor can he without impunity contract a second marriage as long as the adulterous wife lives.

The Council of Paris (829) ruled in the same way:

That those who dismiss their wives on the ground of fornication and take others shall be known as adulterers by the law of the Lord.

The Council of Nantes (875) decreed:

Canon 12. If anyone's wife committed adultery, and this has been discovered by the husband and made public, he shall dismiss the wife if he wishes, because of fornication. But she shall do public penance for seven years. Her husband, however, cannot take another wife by any means as long as she lives.

A final footnote: Pope Celestine III (1191–1198) ratified a diocesan decision which permitted a woman to remarry after her husband had become an apostate from the Faith. His successor, Innocent III, said that apostasy was not a ground for divorce "in spite of the fact that a certain predecessor of Ours apparently thought otherwise."

So there you have it—legislation for and against divorce and remarriage in the same Christian Church. You will note that all the Synods mentioned are Western Synods, because divorce and remarriage have always been allowed in the Eastern Church even before the split from Rome.

The comment of these writers?

Official teaching changes, practice changes, legislation changes, because all these things are variables in the Church. What we have suggested in this book goes only a short way towards matching the broad tolerances of other days. We assert that our proposals have the virtue of extreme moderation and make a sane concession to the art of the possible.

Now let's look at one of the things that appears—but only appears!—to make the possible impossible—the decision of the Council of Trent. So prepare yourselves for a little discursive history.

25
DIVORCE AND THE COUNCIL OF TRENT

Many people in the Church, bishops, priests and laity, believe that the question of divorce and remarriage in the Church was finally closed by the decree of the Council of Trent formulated and passed on November 11, 1563.

Many of these believers, we suggest, wouldn't recognize the decree if they saw it. A silly statement? Not really. Let's test it. Here are two versions of the decree. Which is the authentic one?

<table>
<tr><td>

VERSION 1

If anyone shall say that marriage can be dissolved because of adultery of the other spouse, and that both spouses, or at least the innocent one who was not the cause of the adultery, are permitted to contract another marriage while the other spouse is alive; and that he who takes another, having dismissed the adulteress, or she who marries another, having dismissed the

</td><td>

VERSION 2

If anyone shall say that the Church errs when she taught or teaches, in accordance with evangelical and apostolic doctrine, that the bond of marriage cannot be dissolved because of adultery of either spouse; and that neither of them, not even the innocent one who was not the cause of the adultery, can contract another marriage while the other spouse is living; and that he

</td></tr>
</table>

adulterer, does not commit adultery, let him be anathema.

who has taken another after dismissing the adulteress; and she who has married another after dismissing the adulterer, commits adultery, let him be anathema.

Both versions are authentic. Version 1 is that which was submitted to the Council but was rejected. Version 2 is that which was finally agreed and promulgated.

The reasons for the change and the significance of it are the subject of this little *discursus*.

The general purpose of the Council of Trent was to reform the Church from within and to define her position against the conflicting doctrines of the protestant reformers.

On the marriage question, two main issues were at stake: the exclusive right of the Church to determine the validity of Christian marriage, and her right to regulate its norms without the intervention of the secular state. Both these rights pre-empt against any secular intervention in the question of divorce and remarriage.

In order to separate marriage from civil interference, and to abolish the prevalent practice of clandestine marriage, the Council prescribed an obligatory Church form, without which the marriage would be invalid. This prescription was embodied in the decree *Tametsi*, which is what binds Catholics today and prevents them from getting married in a register office.

To cope directly with the divorce question, Version 1 of the decree was drafted and submitted to the Council.

There was immediate and hostile dissent. One group of bishops headed by Pietro Laudi, Archbishop of Crete, rejected the document out of hand because they saw it as a condemnation of the doctrine and practice of the Fathers—which it obviously was! The Archbishop of Granada phrased it bluntly: *"Non placet igitur ut Sancti Doctores damnentur."*

Another group was prepared to compromise if the anathema and the condemnation of the Fathers and of the current Greek practice were removed. One of this group was Giovanni Castagna, Archbishop of Rossano, who later became Pope Urban VII—and died twelve days after his election!

The Bishop of Segovia, Martin de Ayala, refused to accept the condemnation of the Fathers but proposed a subtle compromise: a statement that "the Church did not err in teaching the indissolubility of marriage." In other words, she would not be doctrinally wrong in teaching a more rigorous opinion than a more liberal one! The Bishop of Modena, Egidio Foscarari, proposed that the anathema should be directed only at those who denied the Church's *right* to prohibit remarriage after divorce for adultery. This was a subtle one too. It left the doctrinal question open, left the Fathers untouched and concentrated on the legal and disciplinary aspect of the question.

At this stage the secular state moved into the picture in the shape of the Ambassadors of the Most Serene Republic of Venice. They wanted the draft changed to avoid offending the Greek faithful who lived in the extensive Mediterranean territories of the Republic.

They got their way. The revision suggested by the Bishop of Segovia was accepted for voting, with the addition of the rider "according to evangelical and apostolic doctrine." This is Version 2 as it appears above.

The canon was adopted by a majority vote but not by a unanimous one. It still stands in law.

The question unanswered even today is what it stands *as!* A doctrinal definition or a disciplinary one?

Again legitimate opinion is divided.

If it is a doctrinal definition, then it expresses exactly what the Fathers of Trent did *not* want it to express—an outright condemnation of the early Fathers.

If it is a disciplinary decision, then it is susceptible of change.

Our comment? None. The comment has already been made by Vatican Council II in its Decree on Ecumenism:

> . . . If the influence of events or of the times has led to deficiencies in conduct, in Church discipline or even in the formulation of doctrine (which must be carefully distinguished from the deposit of faith itself) these should be appropriately rectified at the proper moment.

Our question: when is the proper time to rectify marriage legislation? When we are all dead and beyond the need?

26
THE USAGE OF HONEST MEN

We have asserted in several places in this book that the official teaching—as distinct from the truths of the Deposit of Faith—can and does change. This is no news to theologians and historians. It may be news to many laity. It should give pause to the rigorists in the Church who see every critic as a rebel and every reformer as a dangerous innovator.

We cite, as a classic case, the change in the official teaching of the Church on usury.

For a long time in the Church the charging of interest on loans was absolutely forbidden as contrary to Divine Law.

The Council of Carthage (345) forbade it. The Council of Aix (789) did likewise.

Pope Leo I forbade clerics to charge interest and declared that laymen who did so were guilty of a shameful greed for gain.

From the eleventh century the canon law of the West made an absolute prohibition of interest.

Pope Alexander III (1159–1181) declared in a decree that even as Pope he had no power to dispense from this prohibition.

The General Council of Vienne (1311) decreed that anyone who maintained that it was not sinful to charge interest should be punished as a heretic.

Pope Urban III (1185–1187) cited the Gospel (Luke 6:35) as an absolute, Divine prohibition against interest.

Pope Benedict XIV issued in 1745 an encyclical letter, *Vix Pervenit*, in which he declared that to reclaim anything but the exact amount of a loan was a sin.

Of course interest was charged as a daily practice. The prohibitions were discussed, controverted and challenged by theologians and laymen alike.

In the end, reason and experience triumphed and in 1830 the Sacred Penitentiary replied to inquiries that those who accepted moderate interest and were prepared to abide by a final decision of the Church need not be troubled in conscience.

By 1889 the same Sacred Penitentiary had laid down as a guideline "the usage accepted among honest men."

Now, of course, the Church herself is in the money market and profits from the renting of money!

We suggest that "the usage of honest men" might still supply other useful guidelines to ecclesiastical legislators!

It is the usage of honest men to inquire with concern into the condition of their fellows.

We find this usage sadly out of fashion in the Roman Catholic Assembly. No one asks the faithful how they feel, what problems they have, what pains they endure, whether they have the justice to which they are entitled.

On the contrary, they are legislated for, written to, talked at, talked about, mourned over, prayed over, censured as subjects or objects of scandal, as though they were the proles in some vast crypto-Christian socialist state.

The Assembly today functions more like a corporation than a family. The form of the family is there, but the family life, of inquiring concern and compassionate service, takes place elsewhere. The faithful know their bishop as a photograph in a newspaper, the signatory of an occasional pastoral letter. He makes decisions in which they have no part. He is no longer a pastor, a shepherd, but a president, treating with them through a chancery, as a bureaucrat treats with them through an army of clerks! The organization has dehumanized him by separating him from the people. There are too many of them, too few of him.

What can he report of them but a statistic? What can he know of them, since he never asks? How can he care for a collective anonymity?

It is the usage of honest men to grant to all the liberty which they claim for themselves.

We find that this usage is affirmed—all too late!—by recent decree of Vatican II, but denied by current practice of its administrators.

There are still a number of states where civil divorce is denied even to those who believe in it and where the denial is reinforced by political and hierarchic pressure from Catholic authorities.

This is an invasion of the liberty of man's conscience and no lip service to a nebulous idea of freedom can condone it. We quote:

> The office of authority in the Church is to lead Christians to that renunciation which their faith demands of them, not to impose it. It cannot make personal decisions for its members. The supreme motive of the Christian moral act is love. And the introduction of any type of pressure, even if it be only social pressure, attacks the integrity of Christian love. Compulsion is alien to the genius of Christianity; and if there is a type of law which is not compulsive no one has yet discovered it.
>
> (JOHN L. MCKENZIE, IN *The Jurist*)

It is the usage of honest men to permit and pursue free inquiry on all matters of common concern.

This is most emphatically not the usage of the Catholic Church today. It is a fact of recent experience, even in the highest councils of the Church, that a reigning Pope has

closed or forbidden discussion upon certain vital matters and
has reserved to himself the right of final decision on them. We
object to this. We claim that our Christian liberty is infringed.

The matters touch us most intimately. They touch us in our
lives and afterlives. We believe in the working of the Spirit,
but we do not believe in illuminism and we are skeptical about
private revelations.

We ask, with deep concern, who is counselling the Pontiff
upon these matters of life, death and salvation; who, if anybody, represents to him our knowledge and experience of all
the tangled issues involved; who monitors for us the logic and
legalities of his decision?

We are not made to be driven to salvation like sheep. We
accept it as a gift of love by a knowing act. Therefore the knowing is all-important to us, and no one has the right to deny us,
by injunctions of silence or secrecy, the knowledge of what is
done in our Assembly.

Religion is that which binds a man because he wishes to be
bound. It is not a serfdom. It is the liberty of the sons of God.

It is the usage of honest men to apply the results of investi-
gation and experience to the daily betterment of society.

This is not the present usage of our ecclesiastical legislation.
On the contrary, Church legislators contrive to ignore the experience and practice of all surrounding societies, as well as
the findings of medicine, psychiatry and sociology. In so doing
they disjoin the Deposit, disprise its essential economy and lay
themselves open to charges of reaction and obscuratism.

We quote again:

The continuous testimony of nations, governments, jurists
and even of all primitive societies, ought to be given a hearing
in the court of Catholic theology . . . The fact that all civ-
ilisations, states and denominations, today, while deploring
the evil of divorce, permit its existence, except the Catholic
Church alone, is in itself an invitation to restudy the entire
problem from the standpoint of enlightened Catholic theol-

ogy . . . Even if various nations have gone beyond what
Catholics would regard as the limits of sound statesmanship
with regard to divorce, it would be folly to deny that the men
responsible for the government of nations as well as the
teachers of civil law are just as eager to promote the common
good and the advancement of morality as are the representa-
tives of the Catholic Church and of Catholic Theology.

(Victor J. Pospishil: *Divorce and Remarriage*)

It seems a modest request—an open hearing, a restudy. But
the obstacles to an open hearing for those most concerned are
almost insuperable.

Too many Church officials are afraid of an open hearing—
and for a reason which needs an airing. The reason is this:
many Roman Catholic clerics in high places and low are in-
curably snobbish about the laity. They speak and act as
though the Deposit of Faith were a sacerdotal monopoly. They
have sat so long in the seats of power that they are deaf to the
voice of the people.

A rough verdict? Perhaps not so rough when you read some
of the verbatim pronouncements from our files.

A Papal discourse: "Divorce is a sign of pernicious moral
decadence . . . Countries without divorce display a superior
civilization."

A learned cardinal: "Those in concubinage are in sin and
they must come to the Church."

A Vatican monsignore: "We cannot open the debate on marriage legislation for there is nothing to debate."

A Rota cleric: "I think it's much more efficient to stay in
channels."

An eminent canonist: "Marriage has become a sort of ex-
periment. Many go into it only for pleasure."

A diocesan judge: "The modern attitude results in people
thinking their own happiness and convenience are important."

Another diocesan judge: "Personally, I cannot understand
how anybody, Catholic or Protestant, can really contemplate

marrying outside. They just cannot be serious about their religious duty."

A Rota official: "We try to help but it has to be for one of the Church's reasons, not because the relationship is hateful to two people."

A parish priest: "People only get interested in the Church's laws when the law is an obstacle to something they want."

The snobbery expressed in these and similar pronouncements, in the attitudes of obstruction and intolerance which we have described in this book, is in part to result of clerical training, which still confines a man to a restricted discipline of study and renders him ignorant of all other disciplines than his own.

In part it is the result of a celibate ministry which on the one hand sets a youthful priest, with a set of untested ideas, in immediate authority over the faithful, and on the other absolves him from the brutal dialectic of their lives. In some it is an indulgence of the will-to-power. In all it is the expression of a fear that the unexamined belief, the unexamined life may not be strong enough to withstand a sober challenge.

On the other hand—and let us announce it with gratitude! —there are always the noble questioners, the saintly seekers, the open and courageous reformers, secure of the ultimate concordance of things, who are in the end the true conservators of the living Church.

But the problem still remains: how in the hierarchic society of the Church to make the fruits of human experience available through the law; how to have an evolved theology expressed in an unevolved legal system?

There are those who believe—and we are with them—that a legal code, as distinct from moral prescriptions, has no place in a Christian society founded on a Divine invitation to participate freely in a Divine plan.

But if we are to get a code willy-nilly—and it seems that we are—then the only way to make it halfway viable in a plural world is through permanent assisting commissions of laymen, expert in the secular disciplines, who can challenge with authority traditional presumptions, misconceptions and legalisms.

The surgeon must be heard, the physician, the psychiatrist, the sociologist. All of them have statements to make about man as he is, man as he develops, man as he is limited or coerced by his organism or his ambience.

The lay jurist must be heard, too, because he is no less concerned than the canonist with individual justice administered to a common good. The communicator must be heard—because he understands the impact of modern communications and how their manipulation can change the minds and even the personalities of individuals and societies.

Women must be heard—and loudly—else how can a sane legislation compass the rights and the needs and the special nature of womanhood?

If they are not heard, what are we left with? A vast society legislated by a small celibate caste, self-informed, self-justifying, self-sufficing and ultimately corrupted into a confessional tyranny over the ignorant and a confessional conspiracy with the venal or the powerful. We had it once. We have it still in places. We dare not risk a rebirth of it.

The people of God are afraid of their present ministers. They are—not without reason—mistrustful and discontented.

BOOK 4

THE PEOPLE OF GOD

who have been too long
silent in their own
Assembly.

27
THE DISCONTENTS
OF THE ASSEMBLY

The discontents of the Roman Catholic Assembly are deep and dangerous. They are related to but not identical with the discontents of other contemporary societies. They demand discussion which will go far beyond symptoms and issues: like contraception, celibacy and the curial battles over the definitions of episcopal authority. The heart of the matter is the nature of the Assembly, its reason for existence as a society, and how far its present ordering conforms to its nature and its end.

The laity must be heard in these discussions too. They must be heard not by condescension or concession, but by right. They must not be denied the liberty of sons and daughters in a family, the liberty of free citizens in the City of God. If their profession of Faith has not endowed them with this liberty according to the Promise, then they are slaves indeed—and they have not assented to slavery!

The discontents of the Assembly arise from one root cause: the lack, in today's Church, of a simple familial affirmation.

Like it or not, admit it or not, we are brothers and sisters in a human family. Some of us have been given a gift—the gift of being able to accept Jesus of Nazareth as the Son of God and the deliverer of a saving message for our selves and all other human selves.

This gift makes us a family within a family. It imposes new

familial obligations on us, but it does not absolve us from those we already have. We are committed to a belief in Christ, a hope in His redemptive mediation, and a love, in, through and with Him, for the human family.

All else is method and methodology—a conflict of authorities, a dialectic of theologians, a clash of canonists. We are impoverished and not enriched by it.

We selves are the Church—we human selves in union with the human-divine self of Christ. We are the Assembly, and the Assembly exists for us, not we for it . . . "Who for us men and for our saving came down from heaven."

To make the argument very personal: we, man and woman, have created a family, built a household about it. I, the man, am its head, but not its master. We, the selves in family, are the primal assembly. We have a mutual need of care, respect and love. We regulate ourselves; but the regulation is to the end of love and nurture. We have, in the broadest sense, a common faith, a common moral code. But the faith is shared in love; and the meaning of its tenets is debated with love and a desire for enlarged knowing. If we breach the moral code, our concern is to repair the breach and hold the love intact. Without the breach, the love might never be tested, perhaps never known.

So we are jealous of the code, but tolerant of the breach. We know that we or our children can so tangle our lives that we may have to live for years with an anomalous situation—a bad marriage, a liaison, an illegitimate child. We do not drive out the offenders. We do not pass draconic judgments, impose lifelong sanctions. The self—the thing God made—has to be preserved and helped to grow to the fullest maturity—salvation—of which it is capable.

The Roman Catholic Assembly does not presently function as a Christian family, because communication within it has been broken down. We have no voice in the Assembly of selves.

De facto, our true relationship is denied: self-to-God, in

union with the other selves who have the same relationship.

The Church, centered in Rome, has succumbed to typically Roman illusions: that order can be imposed by legislation, that faith can be kept pure by multiplying definitions, that unity is best preserved by centralization, that authority must be as jealously guarded, as sedulously inflated, as the numen of the ancient emperors.

Family experience, community experience point to quite opposite conclusions. When laws are multiplied, the law falls into disrepute. Language is an imperfect instrument of communication and we are forced constantly to supplement its imperfections by subsidiary codes and other modes of response. The specialized language of theologians and philosophers embalms an idea like a bee in amber; but the bee is dead. We assent to a living Christ and a living revelation by an act of belief unlimited by human verbalisms. The verbalisms are unstable and, in time, become irrelevant without constant gloss and interpretations. Unity—"the unity of the Spirit in the bond of faith"—is not necessarily preserved by a central organization of guardians.

Our act of faith is a free assent to Christ and to his revelation. We cannot be forced to make it. We cannot be forced to withdraw it by a central authority. The act itself joins us to the community of believers and establishes the continuing communion between us.

Which brings us at one stride to the much publicized question of authority within the Assembly.

28
AUTHORITY WITHIN THE ASSEMBLY

Whatever authority is established within the Assembly is established through the Assembly, which is itself in union with Christ.

The Pope is elected—chosen—by the Assembly. The voice of the Assembly is the only voice of Christ left to us to make this act of choice. The ritual of papal election affirms this fact. *"Acceptasne electionem?"*—"Do you accept the choice *we* have made?"

Whatever the present form of election—and there is ground for strong discussion about this too—the principle laid down by Pope Leo the Great still obtains: "He who is to rule all, must be chosen by all."

It has been too long forgotten that the pastor and the bishop were originally chosen *by the faithful,* for the service of the faithful who reside "in the unity of the faith." The unity of the faith is already established. It does not and cannot depend upon the authority of the pastor.

The concept of Christian authority as something imposed upon the faithful is essentially un-Christian. Christ's presentation of Himself was in the form of an invitation—"Come, follow me." The sum of His teaching was love, communion, communication—the free gift of the self to the Other and the others.

It seems to us, therefore, that the true function of authority within the Church is to recall the faithful constantly to the union of love which they themselves establish by their common assent to Christ and His teaching. In the earliest Church, the saving message (*Kerygma*) came first and the exposition (*didache*) grew out of it. Without the Kerygma, the didache reduces itself to a system of ethics as unstable as the customs of men in their changing habits and habitats.

What is under challenge today in the Church is not the "teaching of the Kingdom of God" but some of the interpretations of that teaching, the logic upon which the interpretation is based, and the laws by which it is enforced.

The Apostolic Authority is conferred by election. But the nature and the limits of Apostolic Authority are still and must continue to be a subject of legitimate discussion. Still more must the exercise of the authority be subject to discussion and scrutiny—and sometimes to challenge. Even Paul, the last-comer, contested with the Prince of the Apostles on a question of Christian liberty.

Are we who share, as Christians, in his Apostolic commission to be denied the same liberty?

Liberty is a state to be attained and a burden to be borne. The assent of faith is a liberating act because it establishes a direction of growth for the human person, a conformity between himself and his fellows, which is based on his conformity with the living Christ.

However, the limits of liberty, like the limits of authority, are still not clearly defined. In fact, they can never be legitimately defined in any fashion that restricts the transcendental relationship between man and His Creator. Therefore a desire for order and uniformity in the Christian Assembly is not a legitimate reason either for defining them too rigidly or for holding to certain too rigid definitions which have already been made.

Once again, we are face to face with a specifically Roman

concept—that the object of all law is public order and not the dispensation of justice to individuals. Canon law is Roman to its foundations. It is, as we have shown, loaded in favour of institutions and against persons. It is, we are told, in process of reform; but the concepts upon which it is based need as radical a review as the Codex itself.

But how do we, the subjects of a proposed law, bring about this so necessary review? How do we protect our primal rights in a primal and unrescindable relationship? How do we join a vital debate with the ecclesiastical commissioners who are, even now, framing the new canons? We have no direct communication with them, no hope of a dialogue. So we publish opinions, we stir up discussions. Some of us breach what we believe are unjust laws in the hope of persuading the legislators to frame better ones.

We do not believe that every protester is a schismatic or a rebel or a source of scandal. Neither do we believe that every prudent conservator is a tyrannical reactionary. However, we do believe that certain primitive Christian principles must be shouted over and over from the rooftops. The interpreters of the Word are Servants of the Word. Every one of us, Pope, bishop, priest, layman or laywoman, is a servant of his brothers and sisters in Christ. The law is made for man, not man for the law. Christian marriage is the analogue of the union of Christ with His people in perfect love. It is not a bed of Procrustes, on which the agony of humankind is extended by law to an intolerable infinity.

We are with Christ. We are with Peter, to whom Our Lord gave primacy among those he sent. But God save us from Peter's secretaries and their all too manifest rivalries!

29
OF DOGMA, DEFINITION AND INFALLIBILITY

To a Christian, confirmed in love, dogma and definition are, in a very real sense, irrelevant.

His act of belief in Christ, in His teachings and in His saving mission is a total assent—not to what is said about Christ, but to what He was, did and taught. This assent is a completely different act from the act of assent to a formulary of faith, whether the formulary be a creed, a definition of an Article of Faith, or a condemnation of a heterodox proposition.

When a Christian assents to a creed or a definition he is saying in effect: "If this formula expresses truly, though incompletely or imperfectly, what Christ is, was and taught, then I have already assented to it. The rest is formality."

The formulary is not Christ. It is a human verbalism used to define or express an aspect of Christ's revelation in the language available at the time. Because it is human, it is imperfect. Because all language is unstable, the definition is unstable. Because language is coloured by subjective, or local, connotations, concepts current at an historic time, the definition may convey a false impression to an individual or a community.

For this reason it is unwise and dangerous to make a definition the touchstone of identification for a Christian, though it does have its uses as a touchstone of doctrine.

To put it another way: the authors of this book both recite the Nicene Creed, we use the same expressions "consubstantial with the Father" and "who proceedeth from the Father and the Son." The concept of "substance" as it was understood in those days is alien to both of us. The concept of "procession" is strange to us too. Ask us does the creed express what we believe about the Trinity and the Incarnation, we will answer that we believe what Christ taught about Himself and His Heavenly Father and the workings of the Spirit and our relations with Them. Pin us to the words, under pain of death, we will not die for the words. Hopefully we would be given courage to die for the Word which they express imperfectly and in the mode of another age.

It is for this reason that we who live in the world believe that we have often a truer apprehension of the nature of Christian life and Christian relationships and Christian Revelation than those who live out of the world in a protected ambience of speculation, scholarship or ecclesiastical administration.

Infallibility? This is far less relevant to us than those outside the Assembly or those inside the institutional Church will readily believe. The Pope has a commission to teach only what Christ taught—no more, no less. When he steps outside this commission we are involved, but on another ground than the ground of faith. Assent to a principle of authority is not the same as an assent to the actions or reasonings of an authority. Assent to or dissent from a law does not involve our first assent to Christ and His message which we made without the intervention of a deputy. The faith is our starting point and, hopefully, our finishing point too. "I have fought the good fight, I have kept the faith."

Our fight is to see the faith applied in justice and in charity, in our own lives and those of our human brothers and sisters.

Theologians make a strong point of the relevance of dogma

and definition by reason of their consequences in human lives. They point out, for example, that if both the humanity and the divinity of Christ are not recognized, then the Christian concept of His saving mission, redemption, is destroyed. This is true; but we, as Christians, are already aware of the consequences in our own lives, without the intervention of the logicians or the formulators. We know that we must die. The death of the God-Man gives meaning to our mortality.

We are, by further consequence, not afraid of ecumenism and fraternity, as many of our senior ministers seem to be. We find no scandal in the exercise of tolerance and compassion outside the formulas of the law, because charity overrides the law. We are ashamed of that "Roman finesse" which sets the letter above the spirit and makes us appear to the world more like sophists and rhetoricians than the sharers of a gratuitous Divine Love.

We are afraid of the new laws which are presently being framed and which we know will not express us or the total charity in which we are founded.

How do we know they won't? Gather round, little ones, and listen.

30
OF LAW IN
THE ASSEMBLY

The Church has always made laws, good and bad, about everything—from the blessing of farm animals to the use of torture in the interrogation of heretics.

These laws or canons were collected at various times, but the first attempt to select and codify them into a system was begun in 1904 under orders from Pope Pius X.

The idea behind the project was sound enough. Laws fall into disuse, they become mutually contradictory. They require to be updated to changing circumstances. Principles of interpretation need to be established.

However, nobody seems to have asked some important questions—why use a code framed by human beings, when you have a law of life directly revealed by the Almighty? Why not let people live under the civil laws to which they are accustomed and direct them by Christian teaching and occasional interpretative or disciplinary rulings to a Christian way of life in their own communities?

These questions are still being asked today. We'll show you in a few moments how they are being answered. Let's go back to Pius X.

He appointed a small group of canonists—mostly Italian—to devise a Roman code for the Roman Church, whether its members lived in Greenland, Hong Kong, or the Molucca

Archipelago. It was the old idea of imperial Rome translated into a modern context. Wherever you are, Caesar's law applies with all its prescriptions, procedures, criteria and determining definitions. Once you have this it takes only some careful and persistent propaganda to identify Caesar's law with God's law —and that is exactly what happened. And the Romans are trying to make it happen again with the new revisions! Proof? We'll give it to you in a moment.

The Code of Canon Law as we have it now was promulgated by Benedict XV in 1917. It became effective—or ineffective! —one year later. All the anomalies and injustices we have described in this book, and there are many others besides, arise out of it.

In 1959 John XXIII announced that he intended to call Vatican Council II. In the same speech and context he proposed a reform of Canon Law based on the findings and decisions of the Council.

In 1966—things move quite slowly in the Church!—Pope Paul VI gave an apparently clear instruction to the Commissioners. He said that the new code should be based on three criteria: experience, needs and the directives of Vatican II. In 1967 the matter was discussed by the Synod of Bishops in Rome.

Immediately the dissensions, rivalries and confusions of concept were revealed.

Cardinal Felici in presenting the document on reform proposed flatly: "It is proper that the new code should by all means retain a juridic character."

One of his commissioners, Fr. Bertrams, S.J., went further. He stated that the law was a sacramental instrument of salvation, sacred and productive of holiness, from which it might reasonably appear that man's law should be equated with God's law.

Bishop Martensen of Copenhagen opposed these views. He said bluntly that the law was not and could not be identified with the Gospel, that it could not procure salvation and that the message of Christ was not meant to be codified.

Cardinal Suenens of Belgium went much further. He said in effect that the most and the best that should be done was to provide a kind of common law approach to the problems of Christian life; that laymen knew more about the world than clerics and therefore should be called in to help; that marriage cases should be dealt with swiftly and humanely; that personal rights should be respected always.

Cardinal Leger, then Primate of Quebec, urged that every trace of Romanism in the law should be eliminated and that the pastoral aim of law should be emphasized.

Cardinal Urbani of Venice said that the code should be reduced to a set of simple constitutional principles—guidelines for local decision.

Cardinal Dopfner of Munich put his finger on a tender spot; according to him the law should not create a conflict between legal prescription and private conscience.

So far so good.

But the discussion ranged much further. Archbishop Edelby of Antioch expressed a deep fear that any code manufactured in Rome would risk "presenting the Eastern Churches with a fait accompli, with a further latinisation of their practices, and with a reduction of their quite different ways of life and discipline to a common denominator."

Again a Roman voice was raised—in a typical phrase!

The Secretary of the Commission announced that the question of separate codes for East and West was closed. There would be one basic code for both, with latitude for regional application. Closed by whom? And for what good reason? And can any human question be closed if man is an open and developing creature?

The final decision of the Synod? Division and the appointment of a subcommittee to collate and express the diverse opinions of the Synodal Fathers.

The present position? We quote Father Maurice Walsh of the Canon Law Society of America:

American canonists in general are very unhappy about the way in which the reform of canon law is being handled, the fact that it is being done in secret, without a sufficient spread of opinion that goes beyond the Roman mentality.

The future? A threat of new divisions in the already discontented Assembly. We quote a Brazilian canonist, Monsignor Moss Tapajos:

We have suffered in Latin America throughout our entire history from laws imposed on us by Europe, laws made with a European mentality for European conditions, but utterly unsuited to our conditions and mentality. We are not prepared to have this process repeated once more; and if it is, the laws will not be observed, because our totally different cultural and social situations and needs make the observance of European laws impossible. We can consequently never again accept a law in the preparation of which we have not been vitally involved. And the law itself should simply be a fundamental or constitutional law covering general principles, with everything else left to the local Churches.

The Faithful? Us? You and me and the girl next door? Our opinion has not been asked. We are in dissent—many of us—from the present code. We may dissent from the new one too. At least we have to reserve our rights in the matter. But a dissenting opinion is not enough. How can we, how must we act in Christian dissent?

This, good readers, is the moment of truth. Do we walk out of the Assembly, believing it corrupted beyond all hope? Do we stay in it and fight—because fight we must!—to clean the house and hold it clean, a fit dwelling place for the sons and daughters of the One Father?

31

DISSENT BY
THE PEOPLE
OF GOD

A violent man invades our persons; we are permitted to kill him to defend the only thing we are or have—ourselves.

A ruler orders us to recant that in which we believe; we are commanded to die for our belief and the Church will give us the palm of martyrdom.

A group of nameless canonists, working in secret, devises a law which abrogates our liberty as persons, the liberty of our brothers, our free access to the sacramental life of the Assembly, our private relationship with our wives—and we are bound to obey under pain of sin or censure?

Clearly a nonsense. Yet it is to this nonsense we are committed by the present Code of Canon Law, and to which we may be committed again by the new one.

Our bishop is the appointed shepherd and teacher of our Assembly. Our bishop has caused a priest to be imprisoned because he made a Christian protest against the tyranny of a dictatorial state—it happened this year in Spain! We are still to regard him as our shepherd, to seek no recourse against him and to make no public protest?

Another nonsense. Yet this nonsense is specified by canons which make the offending bishop the final arbiter in his own case and sanction us if we attempt to indict him.

No human authority stretches so far that it can oblige us to accept an untruth as true, to accept an injustice as just, to abrogate our right and our duty to protest a wrongdoing.

Our Lord Himself set charity above all law and all visible confessions and communions. He protected the woman taken in adultery against the penalties of the Mosaic Law. He praised the outsider, the Samaritan, as the true brother because he performed the duties of brotherhood upon a stricken wayfarer. Defying legal custom, He purged the Temple in anger of traders and moneychangers. He broke bread and drank wine in love, with tax farmers and prostitutes and the outcasts of His society.

What law, by whomsoever devised and promulgated, can forbid us to imitate His protest or His charity?

Christ the man was a Jew in dissent—a formal heretic. He was also God in assent to the goodness of His Own creation, and of man its noblest evolution. His stance prescribes our own. We are bound to Him and to none other.

Only through this bond can our justice be more abundant than that of our own scribes and pharisees.

Our stance is prescribed. The prescription was confirmed in the words of the Fathers of Vatican II:

> 33. The laity are gathered together in the People of God and make up the Body of Christ under one Head. Whoever they are, they are called upon, as living members, to expend all their energy for the growth of the Church and its continuous sanctification.
> (Dogmatic Constitution of the Church, Ch. IV)

The contingencies, however, were not envisaged: the fact that bad laws exist, that channels of hierarchic communication may be clogged or closed, that there are good bishops and bad ones, clever ones and stupid ones, and that the bureaucracy is still ruled by ancient men jealous of the power they hold.

So the Christian mission inevitably involves dissent, protest and positive action.

The Assembly of the People of God is not a democracy—granted. It is not an oligarchy either. It is a theocracy with Christ as its head and a commission to save people—not forms and institutions and official dignities.

Those who demand for the Church an unlimited juridical control over every aspect of human life cannot, in our view, maintain this as a Christian position. If they do maintain it, they destroy the Christian option, the free choice upon which salvation is founded.

The mission of the Church is to deliver the message as it was delivered to her and to demonstrate by living witness—not by juridicial enforcement—how it may be applied in the diverse circumstances of human life. Beyond this she has no mandate, because Christ gave no mandate of enforcement. If He did, then we are faced with the unthinkable conclusion that His mandate justified the massacres of the Cathari and the ritual burning of heretics and the expulsion of Jews and the torture chambers of the Inquisitors.

Yet all these things were justified in their time. St. Robert Bellarmine signed the death warrant of Giordano Bruno. Had we written then as we write now, we would have been burned like Bruno in the Field of Flowers. How else were these monstrous practices abolished than by protest and revolt and the defection of good men from a family they had once loved and respected?

We want no more defections, but we will have them if our legislators continue to overstep the first and only mandate.

Even as we write these lines, protesting priests are meeting in the Waldensian Church in Rome to bring their grievances to the notice of the Pontiff and the Synodal bishops. It was not their own Assembly which offered them a place to meet, but the Waldensians, a small and once persecuted Christian group. They have been pelted and derided in this city which is kept holy by concordat. Those who came from Spain had to come in secret to escape the police of that Christian state. When they go back they will face canonical sanctions and civil police actions. Yet they are our brothers who came at risk to give a witness of Christian concern.

For them, as for us, the time of witness is now—not twenty years hence when our divided bishops and our Vatican bureaucracy have presented us with the gospel according to the canonists! Many of us will be dead by then and too many more beyond caring.

There are evils in our time and in our Assembly which cry for swift remedy. Our young people accuse us—and rightly—because we perpetuate the evils by silence or condone them by inaction. They are making a revolution of their own, mixed up, misguided, self-indulged often, but curiously Franciscan in many of its manifestations. It is they who have bloody heads and prison sentences over the war in Vietnam. It is they who protest tyranny in Prague. It is they who are planning revolution in the South Americas where Church and state still maintain a perilous alliance in the face of mass misery.

Their heroes are Che Guevara and Camilo Torres, the young priest who, in despair of the Church in Colombia, joined the guerrillas and was killed in ambush. They understand this kind of martyrdom. They approve it and suffer it. They read of Synodal debates and Pontifical hesitations and they turn away skeptically. Now is the acceptable time for them. Now is the day of salvation if salvation is to come at all.

Gradualism is a very dusty answer to give to those who are caught into the giddy acceleration of the twentieth century. Confidence in the Church as a reforming force in the world will not be restored by vacillating pronouncements and hedged documents handed down from on high. There is not now, there will never be again, a climate for the application of pure Roman reason to the affairs of men. Active charity is all that will avail us if we are not to abandon the Christian mission altogether. The axe is already laid to the root of the tree; if it shows no fruits of justice and mercy, it is doomed to burning.

How can the Christian protest be made? Only in charity; because we dare not replace the tyranny of reaction with the tyranny of revolution.

The bishop who has imprisoned his brother priest has proved traitorous to the family. He is still of the family. He must not be shut out from its love or care. But he must be protested by open act. His abuse of authority must be exposed that it may be checked. His people must let him know that they find him unworthy. If they do not, then they are joined in his betrayal. If the Supreme Pontiff will not remove him, let the people remove themselves from him, so that he may know from his flock the measure of his malpractice. A great principle is involved here: that authority is for service and not for tyranny.

A bishop forbids his clergy to join themselves with the people in a public demonstration against social injustice or racial discrimination. Justice demands that they hear his reasons. Charity demands that they presume his good intentions. Prudence demands that they give full weight to his representations. But the justice once rendered, the charity extended, the prudence exercised, if he is found wanting, then the primacy of conscience and the primacy of the People of God as the objects of salvation must prevail and the demonstration must be made.

It is idle to expect, however, that every situation will be clear-cut, that every Christian protester will be seen as a hero and every villain revealed for what he is. The saint will have his nose rubbed in the dirt and the time-server will get a polite admonition to read over his coffee. The diplomat will always have his immunity while the scraggy Baptist will have his head served on a chafing dish. These paradoxes are part of the witness. Someone will always find it expedient to kill a man or a reputation for the sake of the people. But the witness, like the witness giver in Pilate's tribunal and on Calvary, will still remain. If only eleven poor men are moved by it, we shall have a beginning.

32
THE PROTEST
ON MATRIMONIAL
INJUSTICE

Before we addressed ourselves to the writing of this chapter, we talked at length with a Nordic bishop well known for his pastoral concern. We exposed to him our own dilemma. We felt obliged to expose a scandal in order that it might be remedied. We believed that we had positive remedies to propose, in conformity with doctrine and tradition. We knew that reform would be delayed a long time and yet that people were entitled to immediate justice. We were therefore in a position of protest inside the Assembly. How should the protest be made? What could he suggest, out of his own special experience, by way of immediate remedy?

He is a judicious man, careful of his words as he is careful of his people.

He opened with a disclaimer:

"I cannot prescribe for communities other than my own. I cannot make general judgments about individual consciences. As a bishop I am charged to teach the rule of faith to my Church and to help each of my flock to apply it in his own circumstances."

"In your community Roman Catholics are in a minority. There are, therefore, a large number of mixed marriages. Do you require that all these marriages be celebrated in a Catholic church?"

"My first concern is for the stability and harmony of every marriage—that it should be a Christian union in the true sense. If it appears that this stability and harmony would be endangered at the outset by rigid and unequal impositions, I am prepared to waive them by dispensation. I urge the legal forms and the reasons for them. I am prepared to use pastoral discretion in their individual application. Respect for the human person must be paramount."

"Not all bishops think or act as you do."

"I am not called upon to judge my brother bishops. I am concerned with my own people in my own bishopric."

"But it does follow that justice and charity are inequally dispensed in the Christian community."

"It always has been, I'm afraid. It always will be. Each man acts with the light he has been given—at least he should."

"In your community the divorce rate is very high."

"Regrettably, yes."

"There you must have to deal with a large number of matrimonial cases."

"Yes."

"Do you deal with them juridically or confessionally?"

"In both ways."

"But a confessional dealing is not permitted by canon law as it stands now."

"I would put it differently. A juridical method is prescribed by the law; a confessional method is required by justice and charity when the juridical norms cannot be applied."

"How do you apply the confessional method?"

"That is a confessional matter. I do not feel free to discuss it except in principle."

"What is the principle then?"

"There are two fundamental ones. The first is that the person must be saved, given the daily opportunity to grow towards

Divine perfection, however imperfect his present state. The means of saving exist within the Church and I must not cut anybody off from sacramental life if they wish to participate in it. The second principle is this: the confessional is the only tribunal where I can truly enter the internal forum of conscience, because the penitent has asked me to do so. If I can absolve a murderer and admit him to the eucharistic communion, I have no less discretion, surely, in a marital case."

"Are you saying then that you do in fact countenance unions which are canonically irregular and admit the parties to communion?"

"No. I am saying that, in my confessional judgment—the circumstances of which I am not permitted to reveal—unions which may appear canonically irregular are, in fact, Christian marriages."

"Once again we have to say, on the evidence at our disposal, that not all bishops think or act as you do in this matter."

"Clearly they do not. Once again, I am not their judge."

"But what about the faithful to whom such bishops deny a confessional recourse which you permit?"

"I would remind you that a person is free to choose any confessor he wishes. He is not bound to submit his conscience to the most rigorous judge available. Neither is he bound to a spiritual residence in any one diocesan church. A bishop is a dispenser of the sacraments; he does not hold a universal control over them."

"We have explained to you the project on which we are working. What is your opinion of it?"

"I have not read what you have written. I cannot judge either your intentions or your execution. You are free men. If you have a case to make, make it reasonably and honestly."

"Do you agree that there is a right to make public protest in the Assembly?"

"A right, yes. But I have the right, too, to judge each protest in terms of its justice, charity and effectiveness. You can't claim a right for yourselves and then deny it to anyone else."

"You are in favour, then, of an open Church?"

"Of course! Really, if you think of it, it's an unnecessary question. The Church is of its nature a community of witness. How else do you give witness, if not openly?"

"But there is secrecy in the Church?"

"I know. It's a bad habit. We have to get rid of it. On the other hand, you claim a right of privacy in your own lives, you have to grant the same right to the rest of us. But where justice is concerned, it should be seen to be done and the faithful should be made full party to the life of their own Church."

It was all sane, sound and eminently tolerant. However, we had not yet confronted, head on, the problem of those men and women, innocent spouses, who were faced with a life of celibacy they could not endure, or a canonically irregular union which would set them at odds with the law. The bishop had shown us how he determined cases in his own jurisdiction; how people might find a similarly liberal judgment if they knew where to look for it. We felt that either answer was inadequate. So we took another tack.

"You, one bishop, offer a confessional adjudication based on tolerance. Others may or may not do the same. But this is only a local answer to a universal problem. Is that the best the Church can do in the face of so much suffering?"

The bishop took a long time to answer this question. He knew that he was being asked to speak for the record. He chose his words with great care.

"Look here! I'll start with St. Augustine, because he was a real rigorist in this matter. There was always a touch of the Manichee in his sexual and doctrinal attitudes. But Augustine said that a Universal Church cannot be a Church of the pure alone. Who is wholly pure anyway? So you start from that imperfection. You know the drunk will get drunk again. You know the girl-chaser will be in bed again. But they stay in the Church because they belong there and because the gifts we offer are their hope of cure and saving. A man and woman in a stable loving union—even an illegal or invalid one, matrimonially speaking—are at least one step further ahead than the casual lecher. They are practicing some Christian virtues, tolerance, unselfishness, forebearance, charity to one another. They come to us in the Church. If we act according to the letter of law we say we'll only accept them if they're perfect, if their union is perfect. I don't think we can say that. I don't think we're meant to. We have to show them the perfection and how far they fall short of it, and how they can try to reach it. But if we refuse them the means—the sacraments—how will they ever get there? The perfect don't need the sacraments. Of course the Church has to be open to them, with all its saving facilities, as a family is open to all its sons and daughters. Don't ask me to spell it out in canonical particulars. I'll spell it out in terms of repentance if you like—repentance as a turning to God, but not necessarily as an arrival yet. Peter denied Christ three times, which is a damned sight worse than some of the things we're talking about. But Christ didn't reject him and the Church didn't reject him, and we cannot reject any honest brother and sister either. If they come to us they are in need and we should bring them to the Supper Table."

"A final question. Isn't what you have just said a protest?"

"Call it an affirmation and buy me a cup of coffee."

We bought the coffee and added a cognac which we drank fraternally. It was a kind of agape. He had given us hope. He had sounded very much like Basil the Great.

33

OF MARRIAGE LAW
AND LIBERTY
OF CONSCIENCE

Our sanest counsellor on this book has been a senior theologian, living and teaching in Rome. He is wise and witty. He is also a profoundly spiritual man, filled with a loving care for people.

To him we presented the classic paradox which we described earlier in this book: that a person may not be married in fact or conscience but, unless he or she can prove it to the Rota judges under the Rota rules, he or she remains married in law.

His reaction was a brusque and angry dismissal. "A madness! As mad as to say that an innocent man must consent to be hanged because circumstantial evidence says he is a murderer! To bind a man to a partnership that does not exist, to exclude him from all hope of marriage because a law cannot be satisfied! This is a cruelty beyond description."

"But the law exists and is enforced."

"Then it may, in good conscience, be broken or avoided. No one has a right to send an innocent man to the gallows or put an innocent man or woman on the rack for life."

"For all practical purposes then, to break or avoid this law means seeking a civil divorce and then remarrying."

"In effect, yes. Or contracting a valid marriage by mutual consent without legal forms—which of course is vulnerable to legal attack, social pressure, and puts the children at a grave disadvantage."

"Is this what you recommend?"

"I'm not recommending anything. We are discussing principles, not cases. I am saying that no law can impose death or grievous suffering on an innocent person. And if it is claimed that Divine Law does this, then I will stake my soul on a denial.

"But remember, we are speaking of persons truly innocent in conscience—not of conspirators or cheats or those who want to invade the just rights of the partners for selfish ends."

"Who then is the judge of the good or bad disposition of the person involved?"

"The Church presently insists that the only competent judgment can be given by her tribunals. Clearly they are bound by defective canons. Therefore their competence is impaired at the outset. It follows, therefore, that the individual concerned must address himself to the confessional tribunal and to wise counsellors for guidance towards a just decision in conscience . . . But in the last analysis, the confessor and the spiritual counsellor advise on the evidence given by the penitent. So, in the end, we are back to private conscience, to that moment when man and God stand private, face to face, and the son says to his Father: 'Judge me! I am innocent.' You can cheat the whole world if you're clever enough. You can cheat yourself, if you're blind enough. But you can't cheat on the ultimate relationship between yourself and your Maker. It is in this relationship between free man and the Source of Being that salvation or damnation is accomplished."

"Very well. The decision is made. The individual, innocent in conscience, seeks a non-canonical solution to his problem. Can he or should he participate in the sacramental life of the Church?"

"I don't see that the question arises. He must participate. The sacraments are the source of spiritual life for him."

"But the canons forbid it. In fact they provide an automatic exclusion—an 'excommunication' *latae sententiae.*"

"No! They provide it only for the guilty. An innocent person cannot attract automatic penalty, and certainly no penalty so severe as exclusion from the source of his spiritual life."

"Suppose a bishop or a pastor, on the grounds of scandal, or because of disagreement with his conscientious decision, excludes him formally from the sacraments?"

"Then, rather than create a scandal or come to open contest with authority, he should, in prudence, seek the sacraments in another jurisdiction."

"And if he cannot do this, through circumstances of poverty or isolation?"

"Then he is, like many others before him, like Christ Himself, a victim of injustice. He must address himself to prayer, rest calm in conscience and give a Christian witness by patience, dignity and the probity of his own life in whatever new relationship he has contracted. He is still a member of the Assembly of the People of God."

"Aren't you afraid that what you have told us and what we shall report may give scandal to many believers?"

"No. I am not afraid. We are all here to give witness to Christ of Whom it was said that He would not break the bruised reed or quench the smoking flax. We are here to apply the economy of salvation, by fraternal service, to all who seek it. We are here to affirm the equity of Christian judgment, when the laws which have been made cannot provide it."

"Do you want to talk about the exercise of authority in this matter?"

"Only in general terms. Authority, hierarchy, pastoral prescription—these are all elements in the Divine economy of saving men and women. I have lived the best part of my life as a priest under authority. I have seen authority well used and badly used. I have experienced justice and injustice. I have learned more perhaps from this experience than from my textbooks. The learning takes a long time. The economy doesn't become clear all at once. I wish, though, that men who are vested with authority would listen more and pronounce less. Too often the Church presents itself as a body which has a mouth but no ears."

"Why does this happen?"

"In part because there is not enough dispersal, delegation of authority. In part because we do not trust enough in the working of the Spirit among the People of God and among those who, even if they appear to be outside, are truly if mysteriously joined to them in the Spirit. We proclaim universality, but truly we are afraid of it, as primitive man is afraid of the tribe next door and endows to them strange and dangerous and devilish attributes. I think this was what Christ meant when He said: 'Unless you become as little children you cannot enter the Kingdom of God.' Children accept each other as they are. They play, they quarrel, they dispute, but they do not hate, they do not make separating mysteries. They need love. They give it and take it without the intervention of law. Their elders are their servants, because their needs impose the service. And their elders are in their debt for the love they get in return . . ."

And there we ended. We walked out into the dusty street where children played heedlessly amid the clatter and clangour of the worn old city.

34
OF MARRIAGE AS WE KNOW IT

We speak now of that which we know. In this witness we defer to no one. We have lived and we still live the experience we record.

Of the contract we say that it is only a starting point for the union which we hope will grow out of it. It is a moment of formal commitment, conditioned by the relationship we have built up before it, by the ideas we have of a future relationship. We believe, we hope, but we truly do not know whether the union can or will be accomplished. We have, or think we have, a certainty of love at that moment, but we do not know because we have not experienced all the entailment of love. We have not seen the full schedule of costs on the contract. We have not tested our capacities to pay them. We have been companions for a long or short time. We have fallen in love, or we have come gradually to it. We have come by swift strides or slow ones to the beginning of a life in common. We are still secret from each other, still mysterious, because we have not yet been mined by experience and by interaction with each other under the stress of living. We make the same vow of fidelity and loving care and perseverance together; but we cannot know what tragedy, what war or cataclysm may thrust us apart from the promised communion.

Of the consummation? We will say now that it is not a completion even of physical union. It is a beginning, often a tentative, often an unsatisfactory beginning to a mutual harmony which, if it is not achieved, may wreck the marriage. The act of love is meaningless if it is not done with love and does not lead to love. Divorced from the mystery of mind and emotion, it does not and cannot have the sacramental character which is attributed to it. Mere invasion or possession or even mutual use without love ratifies nothing. If the legalists are right and we are wrong, then we are back to the barbarity of bloody towels displayed at the window and the triumphant spear thrust into the earth outside the bridal tent.

The ecstasy of bodies, the little death, is the first passkey to the domain of love. But once we enter the domain, we find there are other doors as well that open to hands' touch or a smile or a gesture that expresses a whole bible of unitive experiences.

Of sacramental character, we are the only ones who can speak with complete authority, because we are the only ones who experience the mystery. We experience its sanctity and its strength and the grace with which it endows us to be, sometimes, braver and less selfish, and more constant than we are by nature. When we sit together and wait for a child to live or die, we know there is a sacrament between us, and we resent those who presume to define it for us. When we spend a compassion we never thought to own on an ailing partner, we know that a gift is working in us. When we turn away from others, knowing that we could and perhaps do love them too, we are aware of something that establishes an exclusivity for us, a quality of oneness that we could not achieve elsewhere.

We know too, from the light of our experience, that there are unions which have never and can never achieve this quality. We say: "They should never have married. They are destroying each other." We are loath but we are sometimes forced to make the judgment that they have never truly achieved a marriage. We believe that we often judge more truly than the celibate canonist picking over his texts for this definition or that to fit the wild variety of human incompatibilities.

We believe in the sacrament and in the mutual grace it dispenses. We judge not always wrongly that where no grace is dispensed there is no sacrament—and no compulsion to cohabit will ever create one!

Of children and their begetting: we do not believe there is a Divine command to breed our wives into exhaustion as if they were cattle. Now do we believe that they are to be rested and restored by a deprivation of the tenderness and sexual love they need and we need too. We have been given a grace of respect one for the other. We have learned the limits to which motion can be stretched and love expended, and burdens carried. We need the holidays of loving without care, because we care and are careful for the union we have established. To those who chide us, unknowing, for sensuality and irresponsibility, we answer that they cannot judge because they do not share our exclusive sacrament.

We cannot even share the sacrament of our married children. How can anyone intrude into ours?

Of indissolubility we say, as a matter of experience, that it resides in the commitment we have made to each other. If we did not make a whole commitment, then the sacrament was frustrated from the beginning. If we did so commit, each to each, then nothing will unbind us. In this domain we are beyond the reach of law. If we are not resident in this domain, then we are already unbound.

Love is the essence of every sacrament: of Baptism, which admits us to the family of the People of God, of Penance, which extends a loving pardon for delinquency, of the Eucharist through which Christ communicates Himself in a loving assembly, of orders in which a man is dedicated to ministry of love . . .

If this is not true, then the sacraments are sterile forms, fit subject for the sterile regulation of the legalists.

Of the breakup of marriage we say this: it is always a confession of failure—failure to achieve the mysterious union of love which was the promise of the contract. But we cannot bring ourselves to say, with any sincerity, that this is the only human failure which does not deserve a second chance. There are too many imponderables involved to make so brutal a judgment. There are too many stresses and strains, too many confusions and ignorances in men and women, to damn them, innocent and guilty alike, after one failure, to a destructive and inhuman solitude. The idea is as repugnant to us as the terrible vision of St. Augustine of the vast mass of the damned who were shut out by the God who made them, simply because they had never been baptized. We cannot see that we are bound to it by Faith, and we are supported by the tolerant charity of the early Fathers and by the opinions of theologians and pastors today.

We do not preach license. On the contrary, we are concerned for the stability of marriage. We are, however, more concerned for the saving of persons, and of their dignities and their capacities to live a full human life—because a full human life is the Divine plan for them.

To say that the plan must be perfectly realized is to posit an impossibility.

Man is bound to perform that which he can in the economy of salvation. To exact more is to create a tyranny. To claim that all men are given the same gift in equal measure is to contradict the Gospel. If the mercy is measureless, how can we limit it so stringently as we do now?

Of mixed marriages we say that they must begin with a loving recognition of equality. How can we give witness to the universal love of Christ if our laws discriminate against any of His children from whatever communion? The gifts of Faith, Hope and Charity are given to us to spend on all. They are not to be wrapped in a napkin and buried against a possible diminution or contamination. Christ is communicated through us who are joined to Him; we have no charge to break the communication. The Christian mysteries do not dispense us from the natural mystery of brotherhood in the human clan. We are all members, one of another. There cannot be in-brothers and out-brothers.

Of uncanonical marriages we know a great deal. Some of our friends have contracted them for one set of reasons or another. We give witness out of our own experience that many of these marriages are more Christian in nature and aspect than some very canonical unions we wot of.

Husband and wife live in fidelity and affection. They give their children love and care and religious upbringing. They dispense charity to others. The fruits of their lives are good. They are known to be good. They are seen to be good. Many of them wish to be visibly rejoined to the Assembly of the People of God.

As things stand now—unless they are prepared or encouraged to make a private judgment of their own condition—they cannot do it, except under morally impossible conditions of separation or the nonsense of the brother-and-sister act. We want them brought back. We want them communicating with us, as whole brothers and sisters. Their absence is a shame and a grief to us. We say that what they have suffered is penance enough—if indeed they ever merited penance at all! We say that Christian tolerances are provided for their return and that these tolerances must be brought into active play now, not by dissimulation but by that condescension which expresses the Godly principle of equity.

Of sexual deviations we are more than a little aware. We know how destructive they can be in a marital relationship. We deprecate in the strongest terms the clinical inquisitions imposed by the present canons, especially on women who suffer in a deviate situation. We depose that such inquisitions degrade the dignity of the Church as well as the dignity of the persons. We claim that here the widest discretions must be exercised in counsel and confessional advice and matrimonial decision.

But, in respect of the deviates themselves, we urge, in the strongest terms, their need of love and understanding and Christian solicitude. We are a long way yet from understanding the intricate chemistry of the body and the psychic preconditioning to aberration. All we do know is that every man has his own share in the saving economy, and that the sharing must be made known and open to him in charity. Deviation is not of itself delinquency. But delinquency can be created by default of love—and the guilt of that may lie on our own doorstep.

If we are required, and we sometimes are, to express social judgments, we are prepared to say that any relationship which contains an element of love and unselfishness is this much better than the callous exploitation of one human being by another.

Once again it is a question of the moral possibility which is open to a given human being in a given time and circumstance. He is obliged to choose the best available. To exclude him from the saving communion because he has not attained to an unattainable perfection is to commit a crime against him. Teilhard de Chardin's definition of evolution—God making things make themselves—holds good in the transcendental order too.

Of sexual patterns in our society, we testify—rather needlessly!—to a considerable license. We testify also to the terrible loneliness of the individual in this gregarious but shifting society, to the destructive influence of consumer advertising in its exploitation of every human insecurity.

The young are urged to be impossibly beautiful, impossibly sexual, impossibly swinging, impossibly involved—and too many end by being intolerably lonely. The not so young are victims too; so that the act of love is often times an act of desperation and the love affair often is an affair of search and disappointment and renewed solitude.

Knowing all this, being involved in all this through our growing children, we plead and contend passionately for relevance and familial affirmation and Christian optimism, and Christian informality in the Assembly. We are the city of witness, perched on a mountaintop—but if our witness is irrelevant to the suffering and the solitary, then we who give the witness are to blame. We are charged to be all things to all men —not simply judge and jury and melancholy monitor of their follies!

Of sterility in the Church: there is a blight of sterility upon the whole liturgical life of the Church. We use the word liturgical in its broadest sense to describe every public activity within the Assembly—the ritual, the administration of sacraments, the Mass, the practice of priestly and religious life, missionary activity, hierarchic administration.

In every sector of Church life we are locked into forms which, by centuries of use, have assumed a fictitiously sacred character. Many of the forms are associated with wealth, clerical privilege, ecclesiastical theatre, triumphalism, monarchy, exclusivity and vestigial superstition. Insofar as they are aids to piety or identification or associative loyalty, they have a value, but to defend them as if they were the last bastions of belief is a dangerous and confusing manoeuvre.

It is all too easy to censure the excesses of innovating ritualists, who are more preoccupied with the theatre of religion than with its substance. It is too easy to praise them as noble revolutionaries stamping out of the last traces of superstition in the two-thousand-year-old Assembly. Rites and reverences are human devices, human symbols, to express and to aid the transcendental relationship between creature and creator. Like all things human, they must be treated with respect, but never allowed to become obstacles to the spiritual communion between men of good will.

Ritual is an aid to and a method for the practice of the believers' life of charity. Authority is an instrument for the service of the Assembly of Believers; dogma is a codification in human, and therefore imperfect terms—of the substance of faith. Teaching and interpretation represent the Christian effort to apply the Revelation to the human life in its swiftly changing circumstances.

Man is the object of them all—man, capable of self-destruction, capable, too, of self-salvation by an act of love for himself, his fellows and for his Creator in Whom they and he subsist.

The rejection of the Assembly, the tensions within the Assembly begin when institutions are set above man. They will subside when man assumes the place God gave him, sonship and brotherhood in the Family.

35

OF CELIBATE
LAWMAKERS

Some of us have children in the priesthood or in the monastic
life. We are prepared to concede that they are more adept in
many disciplines than we are. We are not yet prepared to believe that they or their clerical seniors are competent to legislate for us in the intimate conduct of our married lives. We go
further. We say that no concert of celibates, however enlightened, is competent to frame even a local marriage code—much
less a universal one.

We do not speak here of moral principles but of the interpretation and enforcement of moral principles by a juridic system like the current Code of Canon Law.

Our objection is based on two grounds: the ignorance of the
canonists in the practice of marriage and their undeniable
skills in the practice of Latin law.

We agree, without reservation, that the married state requires a mutual dispensation of justice. But how the dispensation is to be made is a matter so complex, so particular to the
persons, that no code can specify it.

We agree that marriage requires a mutual dispensation of
love. But who, without experience of the subtleties of love, of
the disjointed, disenchanting, disparate modes of expressing
love, can dare to formulate the most elementary law about it?

We agree that marriage is a saving mystery—which is the

best definition we can find for a sacrament. But for one not involved to dare to legislate for such a mystery is a presumption that passes understanding. What is meat to one is poison to another. What is ecstasy for one union in another is obscene violation. What is worship for one is for another a primitive blasphemy. The best that anyone can say is that the union is the sacrament and the non-union is the nullity. The subtlest definition will compass no more, the crudest laxity compass no less.

A lawgiver who frames a law irrelevant to reality has accomplished a nonsense. A lawgiver, divorced by law from the reality for which he legislates, is in an untenable position. A judge who hands down decisions under a law which he knows or deems to be unjust brings himself and the principle of law into disrepute.

The intrusion of any third party—child, relative, friend, even the wisest counsellor—into a marital relationship is fraught with danger. The intrusion of a law backed with magisterial authority, loaded with spiritual sanctions, is an enormous and unjustified risk. When the authority resides in a celibate hierarchy led by aging men, whose pastoral experience is at best remote, then the risks are doubled and redoubled.

The most extraordinary paradox in the Church today is that legislators who are prepared to commit themselves to the most intimate regulations on marriage are scandalously reticent on the morality of killing, on the right to make war—even a war of annihilation!—and on the crude and primitive moralities of statecraft and money and the manipulation of man by the state. We are not sniffers-out of heresy. We have no time for it, being too involved in the terrible simplicities of salvation. But we detect in this paradox the taint of the oldest heresy of all: that matter is evil and the body is evil and marriage is a concession to evil and that only the pure who have renounced it can legitimately control it.

We detect another evil too, the more dangerous because

many of those who practice it are unaware of it. A tender conscience, a sense of guilt—and which of us knows himself guiltless in his lifetime—make slaves of free men. A respect for authority can, if it is unjustly exploited, make a man vulnerable to the intrusions of tyranny.

What troubles us in the present code, what we fear from a new one, is the manipulative skill of the Romans. Give them a free hand with a document and a set of procedures, and they'll have you roped and tied for half a century to a point of order! Any observer of Vatican Council II and the Synods which followed it will pay painful tribute to the fine Roman hands that framed the documentation and used the documentation for weeks and months to stall discussion on unpalatable issues. If they did so well in the green wood—among their Episcopal peers—what will they not do in the dry, among a loyal but exacerbated laity?

The laity have been much more patient with them than their pastors know. The laity have watched their not always edifying efforts to set their hierarchic house in order. The laity have been quite aware of imposed secrecies and a scandalous gap between fact and Roman utterance. They have not attempted to impose themselves on their ministers, whom their charity supports in sometimes princely estate. They have been very loyal and very discreet. But now, we think, they would like a return of loyalty, a return of patience and tolerance and non-legal service. They need protection from the bad laws that exist and against bad law in the future. In blunt truth, they require it from their shepherds, their bishops who are the only voices presently heard in Rome.

We cannot repeat it too often: the mandate of the Church is to give witness to Christ, His saving presence and His saving message. It is not her mandate to impose Him like an incubus on the marriage relationship, which is perfected in Him and which is the analogue of His own union with the Assembly.

A law, if a law is needed, must be part of the witness. It

must witness to justice and charity—and to the overriding mystery of us all. But how can a lawgiver give witness to a mystery he has not experienced? How can he be shown to respect the mystery if he abrogates it by legal definition?

We are seeing now, in our time, the terrors which draconic definitions have brought upon us. We are divided by the very things which should unite us. We are imprisoned by paper walls. We are shut out from the pure light of revelation by piles of documentation, by decree and commentary and disputation, by law and precedent and prescription, by Greek philosophy and Arab philosophy and Scholastic categories, by Talmudic divisions and subdivisions.

We are tired of this imprisonment. We are oppressed by the sheer weight of print, the sheer clatter of esoteric argument. We pray—only God knows how we pray!—for the man who will lead us out into the light, on to a green hillside, and begin from the beginning, with a breaking of bread and a blessing upon our hunger for justice and peace and a little unfamiliar mercy in our lives.

From our ministers we ask not new laws but a new service of charity. We ask not new definitions but a renewed faith in the old truths. We ask not new bars at our windows but new hope for our failing spirits. We ask not new formulas but a renewal of fraternity in the Assembly.

It seems strange that we should have to plead and contest so vehemently for such simple things. But plead we do and contest we do, because we are so far invaded that we fear for the loss of ourselves—which is the meaning of the loss of our souls.

We fear for our children too. It is for them, as much as for ourselves, that we urge reform. We—some of us at least—have arrived, painfully, at enough liberty of spirit to rest secure in Faith and Hope and Charity, in spite of the follies of the law. We are prepared to exercise our own inherent priesthood to offer to others the charity which the law refuses. But our children have yet to arrive at this liberty and to understand the pains of the arrival. So we do not wish the Assembly to become irrelevant to them because it looks more like a courthouse than a family dwelling. They have become suspicious of law because a law can send them to kill other men for a cause in which they do not believe. They suspect authority because they have seen it misused. They mistrust definitions because they have heard them touted too often by montebanks and magicians and catch-penny propagandists.

Love they understand, and mercy they need, and tolerance and a sense of caring in all their confusions. The pure message they will take, slowly and tentatively perhaps; but they will take it because, truly, they desire it.

The pure Assembly they will reject because they know, from bitter experience, that the pure Assembly is an illusion. The Assembly of the Pilgrims, the dusty seekers, the blind, the deaf, the halt, the maimed, this they will join, because they are pilgrims too, faring through a wasteland, hoping the hydrogen cloud may clear and that they may see one glimpse, at least, of the millennial City of God.

THE SUMMATION
OF THE PLEA

We know that in writing this book we have set ourselves at risk. We have laid ourselves open to accusation of self-interest, to misinterpretation, to misuse, to slander and to the invasion of our private lives.

We have accepted these personal risks because we believe that the cause is a good one and that our case will stand up in court.

There are other risks too—graver ones perhaps. There are risks of scandal to the weak, of scandal by the malicious, of divisions in the Assembly, of propositions wrenched out of context and perverted to base uses. We have tried prudently to weigh these risks and to minimize them wherever possible. We are responsible men. We have both spent more than half our lives in the trade of public communication. We have not wished to commit ourselves to a frivolity.

We have filed our bill of complaints, we have argued it, we believe we have proved it. We have put forward concrete and we believe viable proposals for reforms. We believe that these reforms are based on sound Christian doctrine and that they save the present official teachings of the Church. We have demonstrated that our proposals are modest and conservative in comparison with the large traditional tolerances of the early Church.

We have testified out of our personal experience to the sacramental character of Christian marriage, to the difficulties and the dangers of legislating for it by Roman juridic norms. We have argued and pleaded for the application of other norms more compatible with Christian justice, Christian charity and developing human experience.

We are still at risk because we, imperfect men, have undertaken to plead the cause of other imperfect men and women— those who have in fact failed, often miserably, to achieve a stable Christian marital union.

To plead justice for the just is easy and edifying. To plead justice for those who have themselves demonstrably failed in a human relationship is a far less popular undertaking. Yet it is a fact of history that the great judicial reforms, the great legal decisions which enfranchised man a little more and gave him a firmer grasp on liberty and justice, were often made on shabby cases involving failed and disreputable people.

We ourselves are far less than perfect witnesses for the case we plead. One of us is an Anglican, therefore outside the Roman Catholic Assembly, therefore open to suspicion of confessional partisanship. One of us is a divorced Catholic, admitted by confessional tolerance to the sacramental life of the Church but still an easy target for any who care to attack the integrity of his intentions. But, if our imperfect witness calls others into court with a better and a stronger testimony for our case, then we shall have done some service to the Assembly.

Here then is the sum and substance of our plea.

Every man and every woman is a sharer by right in the economy of salvation. The right is conferred upon them by the redemptive merit of Christ. Any law or system of law which invades this right or abrogates it or renders its exercise impossible is a law contrary to the Divine dispensation.

The economy is based upon charity—love. It is not based upon law. Whatever laws are made must give witness of charity, function with charity.

If this base of love is destroyed, if it is invaded or abrogated by law, then the economy cannot work. To apply to a man or woman a law which demands the morally impossible is to abrogate charity, render the economy inoperative and breach the fundamental principle of equity.

The equity of which we speak is not Roman equity or Anglo-Saxon equity or any human other. It is that Divine equity, that Divine love, mercy and tolerance which permit the fallen to rise, the wrongdoer to repent, the weak to build up strength for another climb towards the City of God. It is our belief and our plea that this Divine equity should be maintained as the sole foundation of any constitution of law within the Church. On this conclusion we believe that we stand safe and orthodox with the fathers of the Church and the great body of Christians today.

The experience of writing this book has been rich for both of us. We belong to sadly separated Christian assemblies. We have found ourselves in fundamental union upon all the essential points of Christian faith. We have explored each other's minds and the meanings we attached to words and symbols and mysteries. We have seen how easily men of good will may stumble into enmity upon a phrase or a catchword and how much patience is needed before they make themselves clear to one another.

We have seen suffering and been privileged to share it with some of the sufferers. Sometimes we have been able to alleviate it a little; and we have been solaced in our turn. We have seen how many decent people grope in confusion of spirit because no friendly hand, no gentling voice directed them to a simple and available solution for their problems.

We have talked with hundreds of clerics, of all ages and many nationalities—pastors, teachers, jurists, missionaries. Some were very, very wise, a small few were profoundly foolish. Some agreed with the line we were following. Some did not. Only a rare one disputed our right to engage ourselves in the question. Some of our talks were formal, most were wildly informal—heady debates that went on for hours after luncheons and dinners until protesting wives closed them abruptly. But in all of them the concern was obvious—the concern for renewal, though the means of renewal were often in dispute.

Oddly enough, it was the older ones who were prepared to reason the more closely, to insist the more strongly for a rule of charity rather than a rule of law.

It was as if, having spent themselves in a lifetime of dedication, they were frustrated and disillusioned by the little the law had permitted them to do. It was they who lent us the most courage, who taught us to delve for the simplicities and not be distracted by the novelties of opinion.

The young ones gave us hope, because they were hopeful too—free-swinging, clear-eyed and spoiling for a fight. But the old ones confirmed us in the faith that was already moving the ponderous mountain of the Vatican, and in the charity that might explode unexpectedly in an already restless Assembly. They admitted a little sadly that the explosion would be a miracle; but then, they said they did believe in miracles!

We believe in miracles too. However, we are not vain enough to believe that this small volume will accomplish them. We are not starry-eyed theorists hopeful that we have a revolutionary document to shake the foundations of the Christian Church. We have made no radical discoveries in history. We have made no new breakthrough in speculative theology, no great synthesis between twentieth-century thought and the Deposit of Faith.

The most we can claim is that we have given honest witness to that which we honestly believe. We have spent nearly three years of our lives in the preparation and writing of this book. We submit it in good faith to the collective judgment of the Assembly.